EXPLORING THE TWIN CITIES WITH CHILDREN:

a selection of tours, sights,
museums, recreational activities
and many other places for
children and adults
to visit together.

Elizabeth S. French

Illustrated by Lynn B. Sandness

8th Edition

Elizabeth S. French, the author, was a librarian and is a mother and grandmother, a former nursery school field trip organizer, Cub Scout leader and present day discoverer of new and old activities to explore with children and grandchildren. She resides in Lauderdale, Minnesota.

Lynn B. Sandness, the illustrator, is a visual artist in drawing and sculpture. His artwork is in public and private collections throughout the United States. He resides in Duluth, Minnesota.

This is a cooperative family work as author and illustrator are sister and brother.

Second Printing
Revised and
Updated 2008

Published by
Nodin Press, Inc., a division of Micawber's, Inc.
530 North Third St. Suite 120, Minneapolis, MN 55401
13 ISBN: 978-1-932472-45-5
10 ISBN: 1-932472-45-2

To my grandchildren, Jack, Allie, Ryan, and Chase, and to all children who are discovering that the world, including the Twin Cities, is for exploring.

As we have discovered, the world has become more accessible, too. Visit America's Story, an Internet website for children and families at **www.americaslibrary.gov** created by the Library of Congress. It offers discovery stories including Explore the States. Click on Minnesota. Photos and a brief description of our state appear.

To my continuing delight, EXPLORING THE TWIN CITIES WITH CHILDREN is now in its eighth edition. Many new activities have been added, previously included activities have been contacted, many visited again and all brought up-to-date. Museums, community festivals, tours, historical places, and musical and art events have been added which either did not exist or had not yet been discovered in the previous editions.

The book continues to grow and change, as has the Twin Cities, with its many rich experiences offered to its young residents. It is again my wish that using this book will help children and adults continue to find and enjoy together these exciting and interesting activities in our Twin Cities area and the state of Minnesota.

INTRODUCTION

Children love "Show and Tell." Our Twin Cities and surrounding area can be thought of as a huge "Show and Tell" for exploring. Through posters, newspapers, radio, television, people and the Internet, word of an especially fun event or place is spread. But much is missed because the announcements are not always seen or heard. Or perhaps it is not known that such places or events even exist.

This book is a guide to finding those places and events in our exciting community. It is written for adults to read and use as an aid in selecting from the many child-oriented activities in our area. Those included have been selected because they focus on the interests of young children...in showing them and telling them more about their world.

SUGGESTIONS

... The book is organized alphabetically like a directory. **A CATEGORIES INDEX** is located at the end of the book. Use it to find an activity like a nature center when its name is not known.

... An asterisk * indicates the activity has an admission fee. Some, formerly with a fee, have eliminated or lowered it.

... Each activity has its zip code listed. Use the zip code maps on the inside covers to find the approximate location of an activity.

... Call or visit the activity's website before going to the activity to be sure the admission fees, hours and days open are still as listed. **THEY DO CHANGE.**

... Internet websites for the activities are included. Look here for photos, one-time happenings and newsy items.

... Reservations are a must at some places. Make them in advance to avoid disappointments. Some require arrangements several months in advance.

... Some places can only be visited by groups of children. Organize a neighborhood group, nursery or daycare group, Brownie or Scout group with plenty of chaperones for these outings. For very young children, one adult for every two or three children is a good idea.

... For groups of young children, identification tags are a good idea. Make them big and all the same color. Do not include name on tag. Those that hang around the neck are especially visible.

... Instead pin the child's name and telephone number on the **INSIDE** of a clothing item as safety precaution in case the child becomes separated from you.

... Most places need a bit of beforehand preparation and explaining so the child knows what to expect.

... Visit some places like a museum or nature center frequently but for short periods of time concentrating on seeing two or three things each time.

... Enjoy the child enjoying an experience and enjoy it yourself.

NOTES

ALPHABETICAL INDEX

A

B

C

D

E

*admission or fee

*admission or fee

K

L

M

N

O

*admission or fee

P

R

S

T

*admission or fee

U

V

W

X

Y

Z

DAY TRIPS

These activities are located outside the Twin Cities area. Because they take a longer time to travel to, it is suggested that at least a day be set aside for exploring them. Some may need a planned overnight stay. Included in this edition is an expanded selection of websites as well as updated listings of helpful regional telephone numbers and addresses for planning visits outside the Twin Cities.

*admission or fee

SEASONAL EVENTS

Some events occur for only a few days or weeks during the year. Approximate dates are given in the descriptions, but also check websites, the newspapers or call the telephone numbers listed for complete information.

SPRING

SUMMER

*admission or fee

*admission or fee

NOTES

AAMODT'S APPLE FARM
6428 Manning Ave. N.
Stillwater, 55082

651-439-3127
www.aamodtsapplefarm.com

Guided school tours of the apple orchards are given to groups of children of kindergarten age through grade five. The tours begin the week after Labor Day and continue through mid-October. Children can see the harvesting of the apples from the trees and the processing steps which are washing, grading, sorting and storing. As the tours are very popular, reservations are a must and should be made beginning in August. Another option is for families and non-school groups with chaperones to tour on their own. Upon arrival at the orchards, ask where the harvesting is taking place that day. You can now pick your own apples at Aamodt's, too. Call or visit their website to find out what varieties are available and when.

A trip to the Apple Farm has other attractions besides just enjoying the turn-of-the-century reconstructed farm setting with its rebuilt 135-year-old barn. They could include the John Deere Kiddie Trike & Tractor Park, wandering through the Hay Maze and going on a wagon ride. Pony rides for children for a small fee are fun, too.

The orchards are open from 9 AM until 6 PM August, November and December and 9 AM to 9 PM in September and October. Aamodt's is located just north of Highway 36 on Manning Avenue between North St. Paul and Stillwater.

Note: Special family events are held on weekends. If the hot air balloons are launching, this is an especially awesome and colorful event to see. Visit their website or call for details on upcoming ones.

What a delicious way
To spend a day!

*ALEXANDER RAMSEY HOUSE
Minnesota Historical Society (MHS)
265 S. Exchange St. at Walnut in Irvine Park
St. Paul, 55102

651-296-8760 or 651-296-0100 (infoline)
www.mnhs.org/places/sites/arh

This is the home of Minnesota's first territorial and second state governor. Alexander Ramsey also served the state as a U.S. senator and served our country as secretary of war. His French Renaissance-style home was built in 1872. The carriage house today serves as a gift shop and visitors' center. The mansion is open for touring all year from 10 AM to 3 PM on Fridays and Saturdays. Tours begin on the hour with the last at 3 PM. Admission is $7 for adults, $6 for seniors and $4 for children ages six to 17. School groups are $4 per student. Reservations are necessary for groups and suggested for others.

Note: Call 651-296-8760 for group tour arrangements at other times throughout the year.

*AMERICAN SWEDISH INSTITUTE
2600 Park Ave. S.
Minneapolis, 55407

612-871-4907
www.americanswedishinst.org

The museum is housed in a beautiful 33 room mansion that looks like a castle. Children should have fun looking throughout the house for the many mythical figures such as a lion with eagle wings or a cherub with butterfly wings. Adults will marvel at the many ceramic fireplaces. On Sunday afternoons special events such as a film or lecture are held. Other seasonal events are held throughout the year. A Nordic Christmas includes a traditionally decorated Christmas tree and table settings. The museum is open Tuesday through Sunday. It is closed on Monday. Admission is $5 for adults, $4 for seniors and $3 for students six to 18 and free for children under six.

School groups of 10 from first grade age and up can experience a guided tour with reservations. Contact the Education Programs Coordinator at 612-870-3374 for arrangement details.

*ANIMAL FACILITY TOURS FOR CHILDREN
University of Minnesota, St. Paul Campus
Dept. of Animal Science
305 Haecker Hall
1364 Eckles Ave.
St. Paul, 55108

612-624-2722
www.ansci.umn.edu/tours.htm

School, scout, neighborhood and others in groups of 10 or more can tour the animal barns to see and learn about beef cattle, dairy cows, calves and other animals as permitted. Guided tours led by graduate students in the Animal Science Dept. are from Monday through Friday from September through May. Arrangements for a tour should be made several weeks in advance by calling between the hours of 8:00 AM and 4 PM. Reservations for May tours begin in March as May is such a popular month. The $50 tour group fee supports graduate student activities.

ANIMAL HUMANE SOCIETY
845 Meadow Lane N.
Golden Valley, 55422

763-522-4325 (infoline)
763-439-2220 Education Dept.
www.animalhumansociety.org

Children are invited to visit the society accompanied by an adult of course between 11 AM and 9 PM weekdays. Guided shelter tours are offered every Tuesday at 10 AM, the third Thursday of the month at 4 PM, the second and fourth Wednesdays at 6:30 PM. A tour of the society begins with a film and then the children are introduced to many different live animals including rabbits, birds, puppies and kittens. After the short program, the adoption center can be visited. A usual visit lasts about one hour. Reservations for tours are required.

Arrangements for staff from the society to come to elementary schools with a live animal program can be made. Some types of programs include Pet Responsibility, Urban Wildlife, Animal Communication & Bite Prevention and Mammals.

*ARBORETUM
University of Minnesota
3675 Arboretum Dr.
Chanhassen, 55317

952-443-2460 (infoline)
www.arboretum.umn.edu

The landscape arboretum is located on 1000 acres of land in Chanhassen. There are marked trails for hiking with one leading across a bog. Each year special events are held. In the fall, a festival is held on a Saturday in late September or early October. In early spring, the sugar bush operation can be observed. The arboretum is open from 8 AM to 4:30 PM during the winter months and from 8 AM to 6 PM May through October. On Sundays, the arboretum opens at 10 AM. Admission is $7 per person with children 15 and under admitted free. Yearly family memberships for $55 are available and include free admission and a reduction in class fees.

Children's Garden programs (952-443-1422) are offered on-site starting in May for ages seven to 12. Registration is required and March is a good time to call for this popular 12 session program. The arboretum lends out garden plots to the children in the classes. All the supplies needed such as plants, seeds and tools are provided.

Children's Garden in Residence programs (952-443-1422) are offered in several urban neighborhoods. The arboretum's Plantmobile goes to these Minneapolis and St. Paul communities with a unique gardening program for children. Contact the arboretum for dates and locations. These programs are funded by grants from generous arboretum supporters.

ARD GODFREY HOUSE
Richard Chute Sq.
28 University Ave. S.E. & Central Ave.
Minneapolis, 55401

612-813-5319
www.ardgodfreyhouse.com

Reopened to the public in 1979, the Ard Godfrey House is Minneapolis's oldest historic remaining residence. Ard Godfrey, a millwright from Maine, built the house in the mid-1800s. He also built the first sawmill at the Falls of St. Anthony. The house was built with the first lumber sawed at the mill.

Today guided tours for visitors to the house are Friday through Sunday from noon to 3 PM from June through August. In groups of 10 or more, a guide shares the history of the house and Godfrey family in the tour lasting about 45 minutes. Special tours can also be arranged throughout the year with reservations by contacting the Woman's Club of Minneapolis (612-870-8001), the sponsoring organization that maintains the property. Admission is now free with donations most welcome.

Children of third grade age and up will be interested in seeing and hearing about the furnishings and toys the three Godfrey children had when they lived in the house.

Children (and others) are asked NOT to pick the dandelions that grow on the lawn. The story is that Mrs. Godfrey had dandelion seeds sent to her from Maine so she could grow them for their edible leaves, make wine from the heads and use the roots for a beverage called coffee. To maintain authenticity, the dandelions are protected for their historic value.

Note: Picnic tables located nearby on Nicollet Island are nice to use for having lunch or a snack before visiting the house. This is also a good viewing spot for watching the boating activity on the Mississippi River.

*ARTSTART
Artscraps Store
1459 St. Clair Ave.
St. Paul, 55105

651-698-2787
www.artstart.org

ArtStart can be described as an organization that provides planned activities for creating art using reuseable materials, i.e., scraps. From businesses and manufacturers, the store collects their overstocks and rejects. Donations of recyclable items like buttons, fake fur, cardboard tubes, pine cones and empty pill bottles are added to the stores bins and chests of materials.

Using these materials, many that could be described as "zany", Super Scrapper classes and workshops where children can learn how to make robots, books and wacky creatures are taught by local artists and staff to children from ages four and older. Fees start at $6.

ArtScraps hosts birthday parties with art activity themes like Animal Shakers, Creature Masks and Fairytale Fun for ages four and older with fees beginning at $120.

Field trips, themed adventure weekly programs for ages six through 12, summer art camp experiences and special community events are all offered by this dedicated arts education non-profit organization. ArtStart's innovative programs link the arts with our environment for imaginative fun.

Call and/or visit their website and/or visit the store. Hours are Tuesday through Friday from 10 AM to 6 PM and Saturday from 10 AM to 4 PM.

Note: Shoppers can fill a grocery bag with materials from the bins for $5.

*BAKKEN LIBRARY & MUSEUM OF ELECTRICITY IN LIFE
3537 Zenith Ave. S.
W. 36 St. & W. Lake Calhoun Pkwy.
Minneapolis, 55416

612-926-3878 (infoline)
www.thebakken.org

In the late 1960s, Earl E. Bakken, co-founder of Medtronic, started collecting books, scientific instruments and other artifacts relating to the history of electricity and medicine. Today, we have the wonderful opportunity to view his collection and learn more about electricity at the Bakken Museum that is in a lovely Tudor style house located on pretty grounds near Lake Calhoun. Children age four and older will enjoy a visit on Family Science

Saturday mornings. Look for the electric eel that is really a torpedo fish. The Bakken is open for self-guided touring Tuesday through Saturday from 10 AM to 5 PM. Admission is $7 for adults and $5 for seniors and children four and older.

Note: Electricity hands-on field trips for grades one and up can be scheduled. The workshops are an hour and require reservations.

*BELL MUSEUM OF NATURAL HISTORY
University of Minnesota, Minneapolis Campus
10 Church St.
University Ave. & 17th Ave. S.E.
Minneapolis, 55455

612-624-7083 (infoline)
www.bellmuseum.org

This museum is a very exciting one for children. Most of the animals and birds are displayed in their natural habitat settings. The beaver exhibit is a favorite. There is even a stepstool for the very young child to use to see the inside of the beaver's lodge. Guided tours of the museum can be arranged through reservations. Family activities are held year around at the museum. Visit the website or call them for a current calendar of events. The museum is open Tuesday through Friday from 9 AM to 5 PM, Saturdays from 10 to 5 PM, and Sundays from noon to 5 PM when admission is free. Admission for the other days is $5 for adults and $3 for children ages three to 16 and $3 for seniors. For tours of the museum, call 612-626-9660.

Year around hands-on educational programs for preschool through grade 12 are offered by the Bell. Summer camps and some school vacation day activities are offered as well. Call their registration number 612-624-9050 for their Education Programs brochure and/or visit the website for details on cost and program contents.

Note: Birthdays at the Bell are fun ways to celebrate a child's birthday. Several options are available ranging in cost from $100 to $200 for a party of 2 to 3 hours. Party days are Saturday and Sunday and can include a tour, games, invitations, party bag and nature printing on a take home T-shirt.

Located in the museum is the children's **Touch & See Room** which is described in more detail in the T's.

The Bell Museum will soon relocate to the intersection of Cleveland and Larpenteur Avenues on the University of Minnesota's St. Paul Campus.

*BIKEWAYS MAPS
Minnesota Department of Transportation
MS260 Map Sales
395 John Ireland Blvd.
Room G-19 MS 260, Transportation Building
St. Paul, 55155

651-296-2216
www.dot.state.mn.us/bike.html

Not an attraction or activity as such but leading to many happy hours exploring are the many bicycling maps available for $3.50 each from this office. There are two different Metroland maps: Bike Map East and Bike Map West. Each contains information on road conditions, off-road bikeways, historical and cultural attractions, public parklands and facilities and touring equipment lists. For current order forms, contact the office during the hours of 8 AM to 4:30 PM or leave a message to have forms sent to you. Order forms are also available on the website.

*BLOOMINGTON ART CENTER
1800 W. Old Shakopee Rd.
Bloomington, 55431

952-563-8587
www.bloomingtonartcenter.com

Youth art classes are offered year around for ages three and up. Summer Art Day Camps are held from June through August for ages three through 13. Birthday parties that could include a T-shirt painting activity are popular. For all the information needed for selecting from the wide variety of programs offered, contact the center for a quarterly brochure or visit the website.

BURGER KING TOURS & BIRTHDAY PARTIES

Kids are treated like kings and queens during a tour of a Burger King restaurant. Tours may include how a new employee would be introduced to all the many steps of making a meal at Burger King special for the customer. Each child may be given a treat at the end of the tour. People of all ages are welcome but tours are scheduled only at non-rush times. Contacting nearby Burger Kings to arrange for a visit is advised as not all Burger King restaurants offer tours.

Note: A space for a birthday party at a Burger King restaurant with a Playland can be reserved by calling a few days to a week in advance of the party date.

*BURNSVILLE AREA SOCIETY FOR THE ARTS (BASA)
1200 Alimagnet Pkwy.
Burnsville, 55337

952-431-4155

BASA offers children's art classes and workshops in drawing, cartooning, hand-built clay sculpturing, among others. In the spring, the Children's Art Festival is held in conjunction with area schools to display the works. Fees start at $20. To receive a current listing of programs, contact BASA.

BYERLY'S FOOD STORES
www.byerlys.com

Burnsville: 401 E. County Rd. 42, 55306 (952-892-5600)
Chanhassen: 800 W. 78 St., 55317 (952-474-1298)
Eagan: 1299 Promenade Place, 55121 (651-686-9669)
Edina: 7171 France Ave. S., 55435 (952-831-3601)
Golden Valley: 5725 Duluth St., 55422 (763-544-8846)
Maple Grove: 12880 Elm Creek Blvd., 55369 (763-416-1611)
Ridgedale: 13081 Ridgedale Dr., 55305 (952-541-1414)
Roseville: 1601 W. County Rd. C, 55113 (651-633-6949)
St. Louis Park: 3777 Park Center Blvd., 55416 (952-929-2100)
St. Paul: 1959 Suburban Ave., 55119 (651-735-6340)

Tuesday is tour day at most Byerly's stores. From 9:30 AM to 3:30 PM, children age five and up in groups of 15 to 20 can tour the store. Reservations are a must. A food expert, "Foodie", likes to plan a tour around a certain topic such as nutrition or the buying of food or careers of people who work in a food store or what you can find in a supermarket. The live lobster tank and the cake decorating windows are favorites of tour groups of all ages.

Other special event activities for children have included "drop by the store" on Kids' Days for clowns, balloons, face painting and photo I.D. opportunities. Checking their website for upcoming event and class details is a great idea.

Note: Birthday Parties for Kids ages seven to 14 can be held at the St. Louis Park store's Kid's in the Kitchen Cooking School. Children participate in an hour and a half class of preparing their food with make-your-own-pizza from scratch a favorite selection. Party size is limited to 14. For fees, reservations and other details, the contact is 952-929-2492 weekdays 9 AM to 5 PM. Kids in the Kitchen classes on Saturdays are offered occasionally, too.

*CAFESJIAN CAROUSEL
On the Como Park Grounds
1245 Midway Pkwy.
St. Paul, 55103

651-489-4628
www.ourfaircarousel.org

In 2000, the 86-year-old carousel was relocated. The 68 handsomely restored hand-carved horses and two colorful chariots were originally built by the Philadelphia Toboggan Co. in 1914 for location on the Minnesota State Fair grounds. Today the carousel is housed in its own enclosed pavilion in Como Park west of the Como Conservatory.

Open daily from May through October Tuesday through Sunday from 11 AM to 4 PM weekdays and 6 PM weekends. The four minute ride is $1.50 per ticket. Children under one are free with a paid adult. Free parking is very close by.

Note: Rides on the carousel are free one day a month. Call or visit the website for the day.

*THE CHILDREN'S MUSEUM
10 W. 7th St.
St. Paul, 55102

651-225-6000 (infoline)
www.mcm.org

Upon entering the museum lobby, find a visitor guide with the day's schedule of activities and upcoming events. Then enjoy this museum built for children age six months to 10 years old.

There are five permanent galleries and two traveling exhibits in the museum designed to encourage children to learn through doing. The Habitot is for the youngest. Children ages six months to four years can crawl, roll and toddle through the landscapes called Forest, Prairie, Pond and Bluff Cave. The World Works gallery and other galleries are for four to ten year olds. Favorites here are the thunderstorm activities. In Earth World, an anthill can be explored and clouds can be moved across the ceiling using a pulley system. Our World has a child-sized bus with moving steering wheel and buttons that turn on headlights and signal lights. The Music Studio is a popular stop with a stage, music and background graphics for children to perform and see themselves in a mirror. The Rooftop ArtPark designed to bring art and nature together is located on the museum's fourth floor. Being that it is outside on the roof, it is open summer months only.

Admission is $7.95 for ages one to 101 years. Memberships are also available. The museum hours are 9 AM to 5 PM Tuesday through Sunday with extended hours on Friday evenings until 8. Parking at the World Trade Center Ramp is nearby.

Note: Birthday parties can be arranged with fees beginning at $185 for non-members and $160 for members.

*THE CHILDREN'S THEATRE COMPANY (CTC)
Located in the Minneapolis Society of Fine Arts Complex
2400 3rd Ave. S.
Minneapolis, 55404

612-874-0400
www.childrenstheatre.org

The CTC is recognized as one of the nation's best theatres for children and families. In lavish settings, it performs new plays as well as original adaptations of children's literature, folk tales and fairy tales. The plays last from one to two hours. After most matinees, discussion and demonstrations by the actors and production crew are held. Ticket prices range from $13 to $39. Reservations are recommended. Group rates are available (612-872-5166). Contact the theatre or visit the website for current productions and dates and times of performances.

*CIRCUS JUVENTAS
1270 Montreal Ave.
St. Paul, 55116

651-699-8229
www.circusjuventas.org

Founded in 1994, this is a performing arts youth circus school for ages three and up. Circus skills taught to the very young begin with acrobatics, juggling and creative movement. Classes are held Monday through Saturday with fees beginning at $120.

Their spectacular annual big shows are held at the Circus Juventas Big Top during the first two weeks in August. The performance combines storytelling with aerial stunts and acrobatics in the tradition of the famous touring Cirque du Soleil troupe. Ticket prices begin at $12.50 for adults and are $10 for children ages three to ten. Discounts are available for groups of 25 or more.

COMO PARK'S MARJORIE MCNEELY CONSERVATORY
Midway Pkwy. & Kaufman Dr.
St. Paul, 55103

651-487-8201 or 651-487-8200 (infoline)
www.comozooconservatory.org

The conservatory is open 365 days of the year with hours from 10 AM to 4 PM during the winter months and 10 AM to 6 PM the rest of the year. There are five main rooms, the palm dome, the sunken gardens, the fern room, the bonsai display and the North Wing for the tropical fruit and flowering plants. Children especially enjoy the sight of grapefruit and oranges growing on the trees in the tropical room and the large goldfish swimming in the sunken garden ponds. Admission is now free. Suggested donations of $2 for adults and $1 for children are greatly appreciated.

Spectacular seasonal flower displays in the sunken gardens are a must to see. The poinsettias during the winter holidays and the tulips and other flowering bulbs during the springtime are especially cheerful. Bring the camera.

Note: Como Ordway Memorial Japanese Garden
www.comozooconservatory.org/conservatory/explore_japanesegarden.html
The gardens can be visited beginning early in May and continuing into September. The Annual Lantern Lighting Festival in August is a family celebration of Japanese culture. During the lantern lighting ceremony, six stone lanterns and floating paper lanterns are lit. And for children, many craft activities are planned.

COMO PARK ZOO
1225 Estabrook Dr.
St. Paul, 55103

651-487-8201 or 651-487-8200 (infoline)
www.comozooconservatory.org/zoo

A favorite of our family all year round. During the winter months the zoo grounds and buildings are open from 10 AM to 4 PM. During the summer months the zoo grounds and buildings are open from 10 AM to 6 PM.

There are many animals for children to see including Sparky, the sea lion, who performs several times daily during the summer in the Aquatic Building, the gorillas in the Primate Building and the giraffes in the African Hoofed Stock exhibit.

The new Visitor's Center, opened in 2005, is the primary entrance to the Zoo and Conservatory. Located between the Conservatory and the carousel, it is staffed during building hours of 10 AM to 4 PM winter months and 10 AM to 6 PM summer months

The Education Department (651-487-8272) is the contact point for classes, group tours, field trips and other programs and activities. Call between 9 AM and 5 PM to talk to the staff or leave a message.

*COMO TOWN AMUSEMENT PARK
Midway Pkwy.
St. Paul, 55103

651-487-2121
www.comotown.com

All the rides at this new amusement park, opened in 2004 and located near the Como Zoo, are for children ages one to 12. All rides, many that allow children to participate in some way, have been selected for this age group only. There is the Driving School, the Sky Glider and the Fire Brigade among others. On the Fire Brigade, a child can actually spray water at a pretend fire. Rides are from one to four tickets each with a single ticket costing 75 cents. Packages of tickets can be purchased also.

Como Town has food stands and carts, planned activities like face painting and a birthday party area.

The main entrance to the amusement park is near the stoplight on Midway Parkway. The nearest parking is in the Wolf Lot. The fenced-in area is open for rides daily from 9:30 AM to 8 PM during the summer months. After Labor Day, it is open weekends from 10 AM to 6 PM through October.

NOTES

*DINOSAUR WALK MUSEUM
Mall of America North Entrance Level Three
Interstate 494 & Hwy. 77
Bloomington, 55425

952-854-6451
www.dinowalk.com

Lots is going on in this new attraction at the Mall. There are 125 exhibits. Sixty are of life-size dinosaurs. Educational information is posted near most. One learns tyrannosaur-rex, the tyrant lizard king, the largest (and most popular with my grandchildren) lived 65 to 68 million years ago in Canada and the U.S. and other facts like weight and length.

There are five activity centers: a coloring table with chairs with a nearby wall decorated with the finished pictures, a computer station for playing dinosaur games, a dinosaur puzzle table with large pieces for easy assembling, a reading corner with comfy chairs and dinosaur books, and the fossil dig area with wooden trenches filled with sand and buried fossil parts that can be uncovered using brushes.

Before exiting the museum, be sure to enter the room with the display cases exhibiting over 40 bird eggs. Note the Giant Elephant Bird, the largest and find the smallest, the House Wren's.

Children of 12 and younger must be accompanied by an adult. Admission is adults $7.95 and seniors and children ages three to 18 $5.95. Hours are Monday through Saturday from 10 AM to 9:30 PM and Sundays from 11 AM to 7 PM.

Note: Group field trips of 20 or more with reduced admission can be arranged. Birthday party packages are also available with advanced arrangements. Call or visit the website for all the details.

DODGE NATURE CENTER
365 W. Marie Ave.
West St. Paul, 55118

651-455-4531
www.dodgenaturecenter.org

The Thomas Irvine Dodge Nature Center is open to school and other organized groups from 8 AM to 4:30 PM Monday through Friday. The center is open to families and individuals through attendance in public programs and classes held evenings and from 10 AM to 4 PM Saturdays. Most class fees range from $7 to $15 with members receiving a discount.

The center's grounds are open to the public from sunup to sundown everyday for hiking their six miles of trails.

The emphasis of the center is on providing special nature study activities for students and others. There are 320 acres of mixed woods and grassland for supervised study, nature hiking and snowshoeing. On the grounds are a red barn converted into a schoolhouse for classroom studies and another barn remodeled into a museum on the upper level and a lab on the lower. The lab contains glass tanks with live turtles and snakes and frogs. A short hike away a large model farm shows typical farm crops and animals. A naturalist plans with the group beforehand the activities for study during the visit. Some topics to choose may include seeds, insects, wild edible plants, habitats, pond life, weather station, study of bees, model farm, fall orchard and orienteering. During the summer, the center offers family gardening programs and Summer Under the Sun Camp for children. Contact the center for a brochure or visit their website for descriptions of all their class offerings. Contact them also for arrangements for a school or group weekday nature study program.

Note: Special events are held throughout the year. Family Farm Festival in the spring, Autumn Adventures in the fall and Frosty Fun in the winter are very popular ones. Visit the website or call for dates and details.

*EDINA ART CENTER
4701 W. 64th St.
Edina, 55435

612-915-6600
www.EdinaArtCenter.com

Young peoples classes for babies and up are taught at the center weekdays and Saturdays. There are also special Sunday art events and programs. Children can explore the arts through classes and workshops in painting, drawing, pottery, jewelry, music, media arts and family art. Some are free. Others start at $7 with grants available to supplement the fees. Special programs and tours are also available. Visit their website or call for a brochure listing all their activities. The center is open Monday through Friday and Saturday mornings.

Note: Summer Art Camps are held mornings and afternoons June through August. Tuition starts at $65. Call in March or visit their website for registration information and a listing of the camps offered. Some past camps have included activities of modeling clay dinosaurs, maskmaking and creating jewelry.

*EDINBOROUGH PARK IN EDINA
7700 York Ave. S.
Edina, 55435

952-832-6790 (infoline)
www.edinboroughpark.com

This is an indoor playpark that is a good alternative during bad weather. The resident fee is $4 per child, non-resident is $5 and free for adults with child's paid admission. The playpark is open from 9 AM to 9 PM most weekdays year around. On weekends it closes earlier. An additional fee of $4 or $5 is charged for swimming. Call in advance or check the website for open swim times.

*EIDEM HOMESTEAD
Brooklyn Park Historical Farm
4345 101st Ave. N.
Brooklyn Park, 55443

763-493-4604
www.brooklynpark.org/government/recreation/farminfo/farmuse.
html

The John Eidem farm is a restored and operating "living" farm typical of the early 1900s era. Upon arriving at the farm, the visitor knows he or she has come to a real farm as it is surrounded by croplands and there are pigs, goats, chickens, sheep, a cow and geese in the fenced in barnyards. The farm has open house each Wednesday afternoon from mid-June to mid-August. Special seasonal activities are planned to reflect farm life and chores for the time of the year. From chopping wood to sampling fresh baked foods to cracking corn for the animals to jumping into piles of straw, with supervision children can experience farm life. One of the many costumed volunteers during a visit said October is especially fun for children at the farm because of the pumpkin carving competition. Admission to the farm is $4 for adults and $3 for children 12 and under.

A very special time each year is the Old Fashioned Christmas celebration with Norwegian foods and decorations. It is held the first full weekend in December. For further details about the many seasonal events held throughout the year, call the activity information line 763-493-8333 or visit the website.

Children's birthday parties can be held at the farm, too. Visiting the website or calling 763-493-8333 will give the details.

Note: Now year around, tours for school groups and other groups can be arranged. A hands-on program for school-age children gets them involved in actually doing things like making applesauce, grinding coffee beans, pumping water into a basin for washing hands and seeing how farm machinery looks up close. The Brooklyn Park Recreation and Parks Department that operates and maintains the farm should be contacted at 763-493-8333 to make arrangements for a hands-on visit. Fees for tour groups begin at $60. The types of hands-on activities selected and the size of the group determines the cost.

ELOISE BUTLER WILD FLOWER GARDEN & BIRD SANCTUARY
Theodore Wirth Park
1339 Theodore Wirth Pkwy.
Between State Hwy. 394 & Glenwood Ave.
Minneapolis, 55411

612-370-4903 (infoline)
www.minneapolisparks.com

Located in Theodore Wirth Park, this is a delightful garden containing a marshy bog, a wooded glen, an upland prairie and a bird refuge. Hiking through the sanctuary and gardens on a crisp fall day or early spring when the buds are just appearing or anytime, really, is an enjoyable experience for all. Open from April through mid-October, 7:30 AM to one hour before sunset, this is a favorite walking spot for many Twin City families. Weekend programs and public tours are available, too. Call or visit their website to get information on dates and times.

*EXCELSIOR STREETCAR LINE
Minnesota Streetcar Museum (MSM)
3rd & George Streets
Excelsior, 55331

952-992-1096
www.trolleyride.org

From early May to early in September, passengers can board this new streetcar ride at the Water Street Station or the Old Excelsior Road platform. The ride is about 15 minutes long with a brief stop at the carbarn to look at streetcar restoration in progress. The streetcars depart every ten to fifteen minutes Thursdays from 2 PM to 6 PM and Saturdays, Sundays and holidays from 10 AM to 4 PM. Tickets are $1.50 per person with children three and under riding free. Charters are also available with at least a two week advance reservation requested. Visit the website or call for all details.

FARMERS' MARKET OF ST. PAUL
290 E. 5th St.
St. Paul, 55101

651-227-6856 (infoline)
www.stpaulfarmersmarket.com

In the spring of 1982 the St. Paul Farmers' Market opened in downtown St. Paul at 5th and Wall Streets. For sale are fresh, locally grown vegetables, fruits, flowers and products like honey and cheese. The season runs from May to November. The market sponsors special events and activities during the season. On many weekends there is live music.

Today, in addition to the main downtown market that is open Friday afternoons and weekend mornings, there are ten satellite locations. The satellites are in church, shopping center and other parking lot locations in the St. Paul area. Each satellite is open one day a week. Call or visit the website for their locations and the current garden produce for sale.

FIRE STATIONS
Children always seem to enjoy a visit to the fire station. Most fire stations welcome them if the visit is scheduled in advance. The fire engines, the alarm system and the living quarters are shown and explained at most visits. The fire fighters like to emphasize fire prevention in the home and encourage children to ask questions about their work. The best tours are those which are closest to where children live or go to school, so contact your nearest fire station to inquire about a visit.

*FIREFIGHTERS HALL & MUSEUM
664 22nd Ave. N.E.
Minneapolis, 55418

612-623-3817 (infoline)
www.firehallmuseum.org

The firefighters collection, after four moves in 15 years, has finally found a permanent home with funding help from the late Capt. Bill Daniels and his wife Bonnie. The museum is in a large brick building with lots of space to display their fire fighting apparatus. The most modern is a 1984 fire truck. The oldest piece is an 1860's hand pump fire truck. Children with supervision can climb on a fire truck, operate the hand fire pump, dress as a firefighter with boots, helmet and turnout coat. One of the most popular activities is the real Tiller cab with video simulator. So popular, that a second cab is presently being restored.

School field trips and other groups should be sure to schedule time for a safety talk in the education room. Especially meaningful is the fire and smoke demonstration using the Graco Corporation's funded scale model house with cut-off front.

The museum is also a great location for arranging a birthday party. The cost is $25 in addition to the admission fee.

The museum is open 9 AM to 4 PM Saturday and weekdays by appointment. Admission is $6 for adults, $5 for seniors and $3 for children three to twelve. This includes a fire engine ride through the nearby area April through November weather permitting. Parking is conveniently located next to the museum.

Bring your camera!

Note: The Minneapolis Police Department's exhibit room with its memorabilia includes a display case of unique confiscated weapons, posters, uniform items and an officers' commemorative wall.

*FORT SNELLING
Minnesota Historical Society (MHS)
Accessible from State Hwys. 5 & 55 or Interstate Hwy. 494
St. Paul, 55111

612-726-1171 (infoline)
www.mnhs.org/fortsnelling

Historic Fort Snelling was built in the early 1820s. Its presence was needed to maintain peace between the Ojibway and Dakota Indians, to protect the American fur traders from the British and to exert U.S. military influence in this area. Today, it is one of our most interesting and well-preserved historic landmarks. Children will enjoy seeing the Round Tower that was once a lookout, the Guardhouse and jail cells, the blacksmith and sutler's shops, the Schoolhouse, barracks and hospital. The fort is open Monday through Saturday from 10 AM to 5 PM and Sunday from noon to 5 PM May through October. Staffed with costumed guides, visitors are encouraged to take part in the everyday life at the fort. This might include stitching on a quilt, shouldering a musket and singing along with the soldiers. Special events during a day's visit might include seeing a guard inspection, a retreat ceremony and a cannon demonstration. Admission is $8 for adults, $6 for senior citizens, $4 for children age six through 17 and free for children age five and under. Educational groups are asked to make reservations by writing or calling. The reduced fee for groups of 10 or more is $4 per person.

Note: The Fort Snelling Museum Store & History Center located on the grounds of the fort is open Monday through Friday year around. An exhibit and gift shop is in the center. A 17-minute film showing the history of the fort can be viewed here. No admission is charged for visiting the center. Hours for the center are from May through October 9:30 AM to 5 PM and from November through April 9:30 AM to 4 PM.

*FORT SNELLING STATE PARK
101 Snelling Lake Rd. at State Hwy. 5 & Post Rd.
St. Paul, 55111

612-725-2389
www.dnr.state.mn.us

Located near Fort Snelling on Snelling Lake Road is this wonderful urban state park. Picnic tables, a swimming beach, Thomas C. Savage Visitor Center and cross-country skiing are here for the enjoyment of visitors. Admission is $7 per vehicle for a daily pass. An annual pass for all Minnesota State Park admittance is $25. The park is open from 8 AM to 10 PM. The center is open from 9 AM to 4 PM and is described in more detail in the T's.

*FOSHAY TOWER OBSERVATION DECK
821 Marquette Ave. Suite 415
Minneapolis, 55402

612-359-3030

The observation deck is located on the top of the Foshay Tower on the 32nd floor. This is one of the best observation decks in the Twin Cities. As it is an open deck, it is closed during the winter months. The days and hours when open are Monday through Friday from noon to 4 PM. Admission is $7 for adults and $5 for children under 12 and seniors.

Note: Modeled after the Washington Monument, the tower was built in 1929 for $25 million dollars. A small museum showing the history of the tower and its first owner, Wilbur B. Foshay, can be visited on the 30th floor.

*FOSSIL HUNTING
Twin City Brickyards below Cherokee Park
Lillydale, 55107

651-632-5111
www.ci.stpaul.mn.us/depts/parks

Two miles southwest of downtown St. Paul in Lilydale Regional Park on the banks of the Mississippi River seashells can be found. Over 450 million years ago most of Minnesota was covered by Lake Agassiz a shallow, warm sea. In that sea lived coral, snails, crinoids, clams and other species of small water life.

Today an authorization permit is necessary for exploring these geological fossils which are located on the former site of the Twin City Brickyards quarry. The preserve area is under the management of the City of St. Paul's Division of Parks & Recreation from whom authorization is required. The permit form can be obtained from their website or by calling the Park Permit Office at 651-632-5111 between 7 AM and 3:45 PM Monday through Friday. The permit fee is $10 or $25 depending on the size of the group. Permits are issued beginning February 1 for dates between April 1 and October 31.

NOTES

*GIBBS MUSEUM
Of Pioneer and Dakotah Life
2097 W. Larpenteur Ave.
Falcon Heights, 55113

651-646-8629
www.rchs.com

Farm life in the period of 1900-1910 is portrayed in the buildings hous-
ing this museum. The Gibbs family farmhouse built from 1854 to 1874
can be toured along with the one-room schoolhouse built in 1878 and the
white barn which houses farm animals. Also on the grounds are a large
red barn, a Dakota tipi and bark lodge and a sod house that was Herman
and Jane Gibbs first home. Events are held on weekends and at holiday
times. Programs have included a re-enactment of a 1920s wedding, an
exhibit of quilts and learning how to do dowsing, the water witching
technique for locating water. Owned and operated by the Ramsey County Historical Society (RCHS), the museum is open mid-April through
mid-November on Tuesdays through Fridays from 10 AM to 4 PM and
Saturdays and Sundays from noon to 4 PM. Admission is $6.50 adults,
$5.50 for seniors and $3.75 for ages two to 16. For a few special seasonal
events, admission is higher. RCHS members are free. Group tour rates
are available with reservations required. To receive a calendar of activities held at Gibbs, contact RCHS or click on Gibbs Museum Events on
the website.

Note: From July through mid-August, a one-day schoolhouse program
is held in the one room schoolhouse for children entering second
grade through seventh grade. Children are encouraged to wear
turn-of-the 19th century costumes. Class size is limited to 25.
Registration should be made early in the season. Sessions are held
Tuesdays through Fridays from 9 AM to 4 PM. The tuition is $30
per child.

GOVERNOR'S RESIDENCE TOUR
Home of the Governor of the State of Minnesota
1006 Summit Ave.
St. Paul, 55105

651-297-2161 (infoline)
www.admin.state.mn.us/buildings/residence/public_tours.html

From May through August, on selected Thursdays usually the last three,
the main and lower floors of the home as well as the Children's Garden
can be visited. Changing exhibits of Minnesota artists' work is showcased
in many of the rooms. On the lower level, one room is devoted to pho-

tographs of former First Minnesota first ladies. The tour will be of most interest to children of age nine and older.

Public tours are available beginning at 1 PM with a new one starting every 15 minutes thereafter up to the last one at 2:45 PM. Tours are from 30 to 45 minutes long. Reserved tours are for large groups of 15 or more people. Reservations are a must for reserved tours and should be made several weeks in advance of the desired date.

Note: Open Houses are held in early to mid-December during the holidays some years. Also Halloween has been celebrated at the residence with treats given to children in costume who stop by with an adult.

*GREAT CLIPS IMAX THEATRE
At The Minnesota Zoo
12000 Zoo Blvd.
Apple Valley, 55124

952-431-4629 (infoline)
1-877-660-IMAX
www.imax.com/minnesota

Conveniently located next to the Zoo, the IMAX usually has several shows/experiences to choose from daily. Happy Feet: an IMAX 3D Experience and Walt Disney Pictures Roving Mars are two of the fine past family shows. Call or visit the website for the current selections and coming soon offerings. Ticket prices are $7 for seniors and children twelve and under and $9 for ages 13 to 64. Reduced ticket prices can be arranged for group and education program bookings by calling 952-997-9714 or 1-877-660-4629.

GREAT HARVEST BREAD CO.
www.stpaulbread.com

Bonnie's Neighborhood Bread Business, 534 Selby Ave.,
St. Paul, 55102 (651-221-1057)
Woodbury, Lightfaire Center in Tamarack Village,
Woodbury, 55125 (651-578-9756)
Burnsville, 1100 E. Co. Rd. 42,
Burnsville, 55337 (952-891-4767)
Michael & Ruth's Minnetonka Bread Store, 17416 Minnetonka Blvd.,
Minnetonka, 55345 (952-476-2515)
Tom & Sally's Family Owned Bread Store, 4314 Upton Ave. S.,
Minneapolis, 55410 (612-929-2899)

Tuesday and Wednesday mornings throughout the year, tour groups for children of preschool age and up are invited to a behind-the-scenes look at bread making. This includes the operations of milling and of dough processing and a look at all the other machines used to make their delicious bread and really big healthy cookies. To reserve a time, call during store hours that for most stores are 6:30 AM to 6:30 PM Monday through Friday and 6:30 AM to 5 PM Saturdays.

GREATER TWIN CITIES' YOUTH SYMPHONIES (GTCYS)

528 Hennepin Ave. Suite 404
Minneapolis, 55403

612-870-7611
www.gtcys.org

Founded in 1972, GTCYS is the largest youth symphony program in the country with over 600 musicians in their six orchestras which are the Symphony, Philharmonic, Sinfonia, Philharmonia, Concertino and Concert Orchestra. They perform many concerts during their annual September through May season. The performances are held throughout the Twin Cities area including at Orchestra Hall as well as churches, retirement homes and schools. Many concerts are free. However, some have a small admission fee. GTCYS have been invited to tour and perform in many U.S. cities and international locations including Fiji, Japan, England and China.

Auditions to become a member of one of the many symphonies are held in the spring and in December. Talented young musicians of all ages and abilities through grade 12 can try out by scheduling an audition appointment. There is a $30 audition registration fee. Tuition for membership in one of the orchestras ranges from $500 to $530 a year. For more information, call the GTCYS office or visit their website.

Young people playing for other young people and adults; what could be more inspiring and special?

Note: GTCYS also has a summer orchestra program. Three orchestras form and each meets to practice once a week in June and July. The final session is a concert for all. Tuition is $175. Call for an application form or visit their website for a printable form.

*GUTHRIE THEATER TOURS & CLASSES
818 2nd St. S.
Minneapolis, 55415

612-347-1126
www.guthrietheater.org

The tours, classes and programs offered by the Guthrie are a way to reach out to children in the area and provide them with experiences in theater crafts and arts. The Backstage Tour, suggested for children of upper elementary ages and older, take them to the backstage area, underworld, costume shop and dressing rooms. Groups are told about the history of the theatre and are given an explanation about its work-a-day life today. Groups from 20 to 40 can be accommodated at a cost of $5 per adult and $3 for children and seniors. Tours are scheduled for Monday through Friday mornings with reservations (612-347-0465) needed in advance. Public tours requiring no reservations are on Saturdays at 10 AM. Visit the website or call the Guthrie Ticket Office (612-347-1100) for additional information.

Note: Once a year usually in February, a Free Family Open House is held on a Sunday afternoon. Visitors can watch a rehearsal, try on costumes, play theater games and see how the stage props are built. They may even be able to try their hand at making a theatre mask.

*HARRIET ALEXANDER NATURE CENTER (HANC)
Roseville Parks & Recreation Dept.
2520 N. Dale St.
Roseville, 55113

651-765-4262
www.ci.roseville.mn.us/parks

The Harriet Alexander Nature Center is located in Roseville's Central Park. The nature area has 52 acres of marsh, prairie and forest habitats. Nature programs about everything from bug talk to night sky are offered here. School groups, families, day care centers, seniors, scout troops, bird clubs and anyone else interested can attend by contacting the center and making the necessary reservations. Fees for programs begin at $4 to $6 per person and up. Information on current programs and fees can be received by contacting the center or visiting the website. The importance of environmental awareness through studying nature is stressed in all their programs including a story time with a natural twist for preschoolers. Pre-registration at 651-792-7110 is required for many programs.

The centers hours of operation are Tuesday through Saturday from 10 AM to 4 PM and Sunday from 1 PM to 4 PM.

HARRIET ISLAND REGIONAL PARK
City of St. Paul, Div. of Parks & Recreation
50 Harriet Island
St. Paul, 55107

651-632-5111
www.ci.stpaul.mn.us/depts/parks

This 100 year old renovated park located along the bank of the Mississippi River between Wabasha St. Bridge and the High Bridge has a large tot lot playground, the Harriet Bishop Playground. Harriet Bishop was Minnesota's first public school teacher.

Take the Great River Stairs to the river's edge and Riverwalk. The Walk, built of steppingstones, allowed groups and individuals to have a message inscribed into a stone for a $125 donation. These messages are fun to read. One stone says simple "We Love the River."

*IN THE HEART OF THE BEAST PUPPET & MASK THEATRE (HOBT)
1500 E. Lake St.
Minneapolis, 55407

612-721-2535
www.hobt.org

From October through March, families can attend Saturday Puppet Shows for Kids in this most colorful and unique building. The puppet stage and viewing area is set up in the lobby for the 10 AM show repeated again at noon. Children sit on the large red carpet near the stage while adults sit on chairs behind them. Sitting is limited and no reservations are necessary. Donations of $3 are requested.

There are over twenty different shows every season. The show is about thirty minutes. The puppeteers maybe in costume and visible. There is often live music accompanying the show. It is evident that all ages enjoy the show as the cheering, clapping, sighing and laughing continue throughout the performance. At the end of the show, children are invited to look at the puppets and to ask questions. For upcoming show announcements, visit the website or pickup up a current monthly flyer at the theatre.

HENNEPIN COUNTY LIBRARY

12601 Ridgedale Dr.
Minnetonka, 55305

952-847-8500
www.hclib.org

Children are very important users of libraries. A child may have a library card at any age when applied for accompanied by an adult. Children's books, magazines, CDs, videos and DVDs can be checked-out for one to three weeks. There is a fine for overdue children's checked-out materials. Most of the libraries offer weekly storytimes for children of preschool and kindergarten ages. Many libraries have children's year around events and all have summer reading programs. Some of the librarians go to schools to talk to children about the library. As the hours vary from library to library, check with the library near you before going.

AUGSBURG PARK: 7100 Nicollet Ave.,
Richfield, 55423 (952-847-5300)

BROOKDALE: 6125 Shingle Creek Pkwy.,
Brooklyn Center, 55430 (952-847-5600)

BROOKLYN PARK: 8600 Zane Ave. N., 55443 (952-847-5325)

CHAMPLIN: 12154 Ensign Ave. N., 55316 (952-847-5350)

EDEN PRAIRIE: 565 Eden Prairie Ctr. Dr., 55344 (952-847-5375)

EDINA: 5280 Grandview Sq., 55436 (952-847-5425)

EXCELSIOR: 343 3rd St., 55331 (952-847-5450)

GOLDEN VALLEY: 830 Winnetka Ave. N., 55427 (952-847-5475)

HOPKINS: 22 11th Ave. N., 55343 (952-847-5500)

LONG LAKE: 1865 Wayzata Blvd. W., 55356 (952-847-5525)

MAPLE GROVE: 8351 Elm Creek Blvd., 55369, (952-847-5700)

MAPLE PLAIN: 5184 Main St. E., 55359 (952-847-5700)

MINNETONKA: 17524 Excelsior Blvd., 55345 (952-847-5725)

OSSEO: 415 Central Ave., 55369 (952-847-5750)

OXBORO: 8801 Portland Ave. S., Bloomington, 55420 (952-847-5775)

PENN LAKE: 8800 Penn Ave. S., Bloomington, 55431 (952-847-5800)

PLYMOUTH: 15700 36th Ave. N., 55446 (952-847-5825)

RIDGEDALE: 12601 Ridgedale Dr.,
Minnetonka, 55305 (952-847-8800)

ROCKFORD ROAD: 6401 42nd Ave. N.,
Crystal, 55427 (952-847-5875)

ROGERS: 21300 John Milless Dr., 55374 (952-847-6050)

ST. ANTHONY: St. Anthony Shopping Center, 55418 (952-847-6075)

ST. BONIFACIUS: 8624 Kennedy Memorial Dr., 55375 (952-847-6100)
ST. LOUIS PARK: 3240 Library Lane, 55426 (952-847-6125)
SOUTHDALE: 7001 York Ave. S., Edina, 55435 (952-847-5900)
WAYZATA: 620 Rice St., 55391 (952-847-6150)
WESTONKA: 2079 Commerce Blvd., Mound, 55364 (952-847-6175)

*HENNEPIN HISTORY MUSEUM
2303 3rd Ave. S.
Minneapolis, 55404

612-870-1329
www.hhmuseum.org

The museum is housed in an old mansion. Its exhibits change throughout the years but always reflect local history. Look for these that show and tell about growing up in Hennepin County and include hands-on activities for children and adults to do together.

The museum has an especially fine collection of North American Indian artifacts and beadwork that if not on display can be seen by inquiring of staff. The museum is open Tuesday 10 AM to 2 PM and Wednesday through Sunday from 1 to 5 PM with later hours on Thursday. Admission is $2 for adults and $1 for children and seniors.

HIGHPOINT PRINTMAKING CENTER
2638 Lyndale Ave. S.
Minneapolis, 55408

612-871-1326
www.highpointprintmaking.org

Free Ink Days are held Saturday afternoons from 1 PM to 5 PM throughout year. Recommended for children ages seven or older and accompanied by an adult, hands-on printmaking activities make for a creative fun time. Check their website for an announcement of the next.

Staff will plan printmaking activities for groups of children ages seven or older to be held at their center. And they will also work with teachers to plan an activity at the center that ties into an area of classroom study. Contact the center for making these arrangements.

*HISTORIC MURPHY'S LANDING
Three Rivers Park District
2187 E. Cty. Hwy. 101
Shakopee, 55379

763-694-7784
www.murphyslanding.org

Minnesota life from 1840 to 1890 comes alive upon entering Historic Murphy's Landing. A walk through the museum begins with a visit to the French fur traders whose life is depicted in the 1840 Faribault cabin. Next visitors see the Berger's 1850 timbered farm followed by the Ryan's 1860-1880 farm for comparison, then the 1887 one room brick schoolhouse with wood stove and wooden desks and finally a town square typical of those found in a Minnesota River Valley community of German, Czech, Irish or Scandinavian descent. The square has a railroad depot, a general store, a blacksmith shop, a newspaper printing office and a church in addition to residences typical of the 1890s.

Since 1967, restoration activities have been underway and continue still with more than 40 historic buildings on the site. Interpreters in costumes reflecting the era meet visitors at the restored buildings and explain the types of activities that would go on there. Food preparation, candle dipping, butter churning, soap making, spinning and weaving demonstrations are some of the daily activities shown. A horse-drawn trolley ride acts as a shuttle on the site and is a way for visitors to experience a typical 19th century means of transportation.

The Pioneer Kids' Play Area in the Chaska Depot is a new addition to the museum. Children can play house 1880's style through cooking, washing and dress-up with authentic wash tub, pots and pans and try on clothes of the time.

From Memorial Day through Labor Day, Historic Murphy's Landing is open weekends for all their living history activities from 10 AM to 5 PM Saturday and noon to 5 PM Sunday. It is open on weekdays for self-guided touring from 10 AM to 4 PM. On weekdays, visitors with the tour brochure can walk the grounds looking into the building interiors through the windows and glass doors.

Admission is $8.50 adults and $7 for seniors and children ages three to eleven. However, on the weekends in June when guided walking tours are scheduled, admission is $6 for adults, $5 for seniors and children ages three to 11 and free for children two and under. Group tour and educational program reservations can be scheduled year-round for a fee of $6 per person. Parking is free. Visit their website for the latest news.

Note: Special events are planned year-round including the Live It History weekends and in late November through mid-December, the Folkways of the Holidays celebration.

*HISTORY THEATRE
30 E. 10th St.
St. Paul, 55101

651-292-4323 (infoline)
www.historytheatre.com

This theatre performs plays that bring to life events that helped shape Minnesota and Midwestern history. Authentic music, costumes and original scripts are used. Performance times are Thursday at 7:30 PM, Friday and Saturday at 8 PM and a Sunday matinee at 2 PM. Matinee performances are also available at other times with advance arrangements. Tickets are $20 to $32 with a discount for adult, senior and student groups.

HUMANE SOCIETY FOR COMPANION ANIMALS (HSCA)
1115 Beulah Lane
St. Paul, 55108

651-645-7387 (infoline)
www.hsca.net

The society offers tours of the shelter Tuesday through Friday for children of elementary age and up. They give talks and show films stressing the importance of pet owner responsibilities. Staff from the society will visit schools and other groups bringing live animals such as a dog, cat or rabbit. Contact the Community Coordinator at 651-645-7387 ext. 103 for information on tour planning and school visits. Advance reservations are needed to schedule these activities. HSCA is open from noon to 6 PM except Tuesday and Thursday when it is open until 8 PM.

Note: During the summer months, an Animal Adventure Program is offered for children of third through sixth grades. The one day program cost is $60 and includes a snack, certificate and lots of activities and games such as Animal Care Bingo. Their week-long camp programs cost $220.

INDIAN MOUNDS PARK
Dayton's Bluff
Earl St. & Mounds Blvd.
St. Paul, 55106

651-632-5111
www.stpaul.gov/depts/parks/userguide/indianmounds.html

The park has historical interest in that it is believed to have been a memorial site for local Native American Indian tribes. These burial mounds, sacred for over 2,000 years, deserve our respectful care.

The park also offers a spectacular view of the river below and the St. Paul municipal airport south of the city. The park has a tot lot with swings and slides. Nearby are picnic tables and benches.

INSECT COLLECTION
University of Minnesota, St. Paul Campus
Dept. of Entomology
219 Hodson Hall
1980 Follwell Ave.
St. Paul, 55108

612-624-1254
www.entomology.umn.edu/museum

Located on the fourth floor of Hodson Hall is an insect exhibit in display cases. On the third floor, an insect museum with current holdings at the time of a recent visit, were 3,403,638 specimens representing 48,367 species. For the most recent count, check their website. Advanced tour arrangements are required for the museum but not for the display case exhibits. Insects big and small from all over the world are identified in this very unique collection.

NOTES

*JACKSON STREET ROUNDHOUSE
Minnesota Transportation Museum (MTM)
193 E. Pennsylvania Ave.
St. Paul, 55101

651-228-0263
www.trainride.org

Our community is fortunate to have one of the first railroad maintenance shops in Minnesota restored and open to the public. This is a train museum for children and adults. Immediately upon entering, the Red Cedar & Western #2 steam locomotive with coal car draws attention. A current restoration project that will actually operate when completed has a sign that reads "Please do not climb on me. I don't want anyone to get hurt." However, most small children cannot resist a quick climb on before getting caught. By diverting their attention to the ramp leading to the many restored railcars and locomotives on the second level, all visitors will find this continually growing museum staffed by enthusiastic volunteers, an attraction to explore again and again.

Look for and read about the 1893 Drover's Coach, the Hustle Muscle, the 1890 Gopher Business Car and the Dan Patch. Take a break and watch the children build a Thomas the Tank railroad line with engines and cars on the wooden tracked tables in the children's play area. Call to arrange field trips for schools and other groups.

With volunteer staff permission on Saturdays and other times by appointment, children ages eight and up and most adults should find interesting watching the volunteers work on the diesel and steam engines in the Restoration Shop.

The roundhouse is open Wednesday 10 AM to 4 PM and Saturday 10 AM to 5 PM and other days by appointment. Admission is $5 ages two and up. Train rides when available are an additional $2 per person. Ride the caboose or a passenger car pulled by a locomotive that authentically whistles as it starts down the track. The trip is about 20 to 30 minutes.

Note: A birthday can be celebrated at the museum. Fees begin at $100 for two hours use of the private party railcar in addition to the $5 admission per person. Train rides and other special events can be arranged for additional charges.

*JAMES J. HILL HOUSE
Minnesota Historical Society (MHS)
240 Summit Ave.
St. Paul, 55102

651-297-2555
www.mnhs.org/places/sites/jjhh/index.html

This is the home of the builder of the Great Northern Railroad, James J. Hill. It was completed in 1891 at a cost of over $931,000. The home has 32 rooms, 13 bathrooms, 22 fireplaces and a very large 100-foot reception hall. Programs and tours are held regularly throughout the year. There have been lectures on its architecture, parlor concerts, 150th Birthday party celebration in 1988 and a play about how the Hill House servants prepared for the holidays.

The house is open for guided public tours every 30 minutes Wednesday through Saturday from 10 AM to 3:30 PM and Sunday 1 to 3:30 PM. Advance reservations are suggested. Admission is $8 for adults, $6 for seniors and $4 for children ages six to 17. Weekday school tours can be arranged for children of preschool age and older.

Note: Throughout the year on Mondays and Tuesdays, a 2 1/2 hour activity-oriented children's workshop is held for groups in grades three through five. Children explore what it is like to live in the Hill House during the late 19th and early 20th centuries. The planned activities include a scavenger hunt, period sing-a-long and etiquette lesson. Reservations are required. The fee is $8 per person with a minimum group size of 25 requested.

JAPAN AMERICA SOCIETY OF MINNESOTA (JASM)
Riverplace, Suite EH-131
43 Main St. S.E.
Minneapolis, 55414

612-627-9357
www.mn-japan.org

The society's purpose is to promote an appreciation of cultural, educational, business, public affairs and other interests which bring the peoples of Japan and our community closer together through mutual understanding, respect and cooperation. Membership is open to individuals, organizations and corporations.

Member events are held throughout the year. Tsushin, a monthly newsletter has a calendar listing their many activities and events. It is available on their website. Or contact the society weekdays between 9 AM and 5 PM for membership information and to receive a copy of the Tsushin.

Ask about JASM's Japan in a Suitcase Program that can be scheduled for community and school visits. The suitcase is really a trunk containing Japanese artifacts, books, maps and activities. Availability is dependent on present staffing. The program visits are free.

JERRY'S FOOD STORES
Eden Prairie: 9625 Anderson Lake Pkwy., 55344 (952-941-9680)
Edina: 5125 Vernon Ave., 55436 (952-929-2685)

Weekday mornings are the best time to tour one of Jerry's stores. However, arrangements can be made for visits at other times for organized groups such as Scouts, Brownies and Cubs. The deli, meat department, produce, dairy and bakery areas may be seen and explained during the tour that lasts between 30 minutes to an hour. At the bakery, it might be possible to see the cake decorator add the finishing touches to a party cake. At the delivery area, it is impressive to see the paper crusher flatten cardboard boxes into large, compact blocks of paper for recycling. The sausage making operations at the Edina store is explained. Each store offers a different tour as not all stores have the same operations. Groups of 15 are ideal for tours that are best suited for children of grade two and up. As reservations in advance are required, contact the nearest store in your area to make arrangements for a tour.

*JONATHAN PADELFORD PACKET BOAT CO., INC.
Harriet Island
St. Paul, 55107

651-227-1100 (infoline)
800-543-3908
www.riverrides.com

The Jonathan Padelford or its larger sister ship, the Harriet Bishop, sails on the Mississippi from downtown St. Paul's Harriet Island to within sight of Fort Snelling. The Anson Northrup, a side-wheeler, now also sails from Harriet Island. Two narrated public cruises are offered daily. One ship sails at noon and another at 2 PM from June through August. During the month of May, school trips can be arranged by reservation. In the month of September, the paddlewheelers sail on Saturday, Sunday and holidays at 2 PM. The trips are about 90 minutes.

Snacks are available for purchase on the boats. Bring jackets or sweaters as it gets cold on the river even in the summer. Weekdays adult and senior tickets are $10 and children ages five to 12 are $7.50. On weekends adult tickets are $15, seniors are $12 and children $7.50.

KITE FLYING
Minnesota Kite Society (MKS)
P.O. Box 580016
Minneapolis, 55458

www.mnkites.org

Dedicated to the promotion of kite flying throughout the state, many fun and colorful kite flying events are planned throughout the year to do so. The Frosty Fingers Kite Fly is held on Como Lake the last weekend of January during St. Paul's Winter Carnival celebration. Other events held traditionally include the Annual Lake Harriet Winter Kite Festival in mid-January and the Flying Colors Kite Festival in August. Their very detailed website lists the flights scheduled throughout the year and includes location driving directions.

Annual memberships are available for $20 which includes a newsletter and discounts on kite purchases. However, there is no charge for enjoying the outdoor kite flying events

Come Fly With Us!

Note: Special school activities such as a member bringing and talking about different kinds of kites can be arranged by calling 763-536-8552. There is no charge for the visits but donations are appreciated to fund these activities.

*LADY ELEGANT'S TEA ROOM
2230 Carter Ave.
St. Paul, 55108

651-645-6676
www.ladyelegantstea.com

Children of five and older can partake of a three-course tea party along with instruction in proper tea etiquette at Lady Elegant's Tea Room. Located in an English Tudor building in St. Anthony Park's Milton Square, the setting is perfect for a child's tea party and Mom, Dad, Grandparent or other accompanying adult liking tea, too.

Reservations are required for all their themed parties. Prices range per child from $25 for the Birthday Party to $9 for Tea Time. Call to request or stop by for their Let's Have a Tea Party! brochure Wednesday through Saturday between 11 AM and 5 PM. On Thursdays the tea room is open until 7 PM.

During regular store hours, a child's menu is available along with the adult offerings for those who want to drop by for perhaps a hot cocoa with whipped cream & sprinkles or pot of tea with tasty scones.

Note: The American Girl Tea Party is offered frequently throughout the year. Always on a Saturday with seatings at 11 AM or 2 PM, the cost is $22 per person. At this event, children are invited to dressup and bring their favorite doll for tea, etiquette lesson and story.

*LAKE HARRIET "OLD 1300" TROLLEY
Minnesota Streetcar Museum (MSM)
42nd & Queen Ave. S. on the West Side of Lake Harriet
Minneapolis, 55410

952-922-1096 (infoline)
www.trolleyride.org

"Old 1300" is one of three authentically restored streetcars that once operated on the Como-Harriet Streetcar Line. Now it is operated by the Minnesota Streetcar Museum which spun off from the Minnesota Transportation Museum in 2004-2005. The trip is over a mile long running through a lovely area near the west side of Lake Harriet. Boarding is now available from three locations: Linden Hills Station at Queen Ave. S. and W. 42nd St. near the Lake Harriet Bandstand, Cottage City stop beneath the William Berry Bridge and Lake Calhoun platform. Passengers purchase tokens for $2 before boarding and drop them into the fare box upon boarding the trolley. Ages three and under ride free.

During the summer the streetcar operates from early May through Labor Day from 6:30 PM to dusk Monday through Friday and from 12:30 PM to dusk on weekends and holidays. After Labor Day, weather permitting, it operates through November on weekends only from 12:30 PM to 5 PM.

The streetcar is available for charter rental. The telephone number for more charter information and to make reservations is 952-922-1096. This would be a unique way to celebrate a birthday.

LANDMARK CENTER
Across from Rice Park
75 W. 5th St.
St. Paul, 55102

651-292-3233 or 651-292-3225 (infoline)
www.landmarkcenter.org

The Landmark Center won an American Institute of Architects award for the beautiful restoration of this 1902 building that originally housed the Federal courts and post office. In 1978 it reopened to become a cultural center for all ages. Walk-in tours are regularly held on Sundays at noon and Thursdays at 11 AM and require no reservations. If a special event is being held on Sunday, call 651-292-3225 to confirm noon tour. Self-guided tour books can be purchased for $1 at the main floor information desk. The tour book is now available free in many non-English languages.

Often there are Sundays at Landmark programs. Concerts and other family events are held in the center cortile. Columns, a Landmark Center calendar of events, lists the many daily activities and special happenings. Call to receive the mailing. Landmark Center hours vary but it is open every day. For more information about events, please call or visit the website.

Note: Education, school and other special groups with ten or more children in fourth grade and up can tour be arrangement through calling 651-292-3230. These reservations should be made at least two weeks in advance of desired date.

LEGO IMAGINATION CENTER
Mall of America South Entrance Level One
Interstate 494 & Hwy. 77
Bloomington, 55425

952-858-8949

Upon entering the store-center, you see the gigantic Clock Tower built of LEGOs. Look up and you can see a key turning to "wind" the clock. In the carpeted play area, large wooden boxes with center platforms are arranged for toddlers through teens (and parents who can squeeze in) for building things from DUPLO and LEGO blocks. Newly added is a derby ramp where children can race their LEGO made cars to the timed finish line. All finish within 1:30 seconds. As all children must be with an adult, benches are nearby for sitting and watching. The center is open Monday through Saturday from 10 AM to 9:30 PM and Sundays from 11 AM to 7 PM.

Note: The large permanent LEGO sculptures including the green-eyed blinking Triceratops are glued together. So don't try to take them apart.

LUNDS FOOD STORE
Highland: 2128 Ford Pkwy., St. Paul, 55116 (651-698-5845)

Children seem as fascinated by their tour of Lund's grocery store as adults who grocery shop here. Groups have come from as far as Duluth to see the fresh fish, taste the pepper cheese and guess what strange vegetable (maybe an artichoke?) they are being shown. Other highlights include discovering how merchandise comes into the store and ends up on the shelves and what happens to a shoplifter. Also included may be information on career opportunities in the grocery industry. Wednesday and Thursday mornings are best and children of preschool age through adults can be accommodated. Reservations several weeks in advance are requested. A treat is provided such as a piece of fruit or cookie.

*McDONALD RESTAURANTS BIRTHDAY PARTIES & PLAY PLACES

www.mcdonalds.com

Birthday parties are fun to have at McDonald's. A meal, cake and party favors are provided with some restaurants also offering games and a birthday gift. Party costs vary depending on the number of children attending. A few days to two weeks notice is needed to schedule a party. Contact the McDonald's restaurant nearest you to inquire if they offer birthday parties or can help you locate one that does.

McDonald Play Places have playground equipment for children to climb on and romp over while you watch and relax with that last cup of coffee or shake. Use your zipcode on their website to locate the nearest McDonald's and those with a Play Place.

*MACPHAIL CENTER FOR MUSIC
501 S. 2nd St.
Minneapolis, 55401

612-321-0100 (infoline)
www.macphail.org

Help children discover the joys of the arts and music through MacPhail Center for Music programs. At MacPhail a child's artistic education can begin as young as six weeks. Musical Trolley, for children ages four through kindergarten, is about the many instruments of the orchestra. Children learn about composers, listen and play instruments and then create their own compositions. For information on registration and other classes, contact them.

In 2007, MacPhail moved to its new location at 2nd St. S. and 5th Ave. S in Minneapolis. Stop by and take a look...and maybe a listen.

MALL OF AMERICA (MOA)
Interstate 494 & Hwy. 77
60 E. Broadway
Bloomington, 55425

952-883-8800 (infoline)
www.mallofamerica.com

MOA has several major attractions for children to explore with family or school groups. One of the newest is the Dinosaur Walk Museum. Lego Imagination Center and Underwater Adventures Aquarium are two others. Look for information on each in their respective alphabetical location.

Information about each can also be found on the MOA website at Kids & Families. MOA hours are 10 AM to 9:30 PM Monday through Saturday and 11 AM to 7 PM Sunday.

The Park at MOA 952-883-8600 (infoline) **www.theparkatmoa.com** is the well-known indoor amusement and entertainment park located in Center Court. Designed with children and families in mind, it is a nice alternative for those days when the outdoors is not. There are lots of trees, benches and walking spaces here, too. The Park is mainly for rides and eats. There are over 30 rides and attractions. The rides cost $2.40 to $4.80. For $24.95 a wristband can be purchased allowing for unlimited rides for a day. Hours are 10 AM to 7:30 PM or later depending on day of the week.

Note: Birthdays can be celebrated at The Park for groups of four or more. No reservations are taken but party must check in at Guest Relations on the second level to purchase the Birthday Party Package. The cost is $17.95 per person and includes a wristband good for five hours of rides. A birthday cake can be ordered in advance for an additional fee. Visit the website for details or call 952-883-8555.

MAPLEWOOD NATURE CENTER
2659 E. 7th St.
Maplewood, 55119

651-249-2170
www.ci.maplewood.mn.us

This center has an interpretive building that houses reptiles and amphibians in glass cases. There is a children's Touch Corner with interactive objects such as antlers, horns and furs to feel and examine and books and magazines to read. Animal programs are held for children of preschool age and older. An annual checklist for recording dates of first sightings of birds and animals at the center is kept each year. Classes and programs with small fees from $1 to $5 are offered. Pondering the Pond is one of the most popular classes. Registration and class information is available by calling or visiting the center or the website.

There is lots going on at this center. There are trails for hiking. The paths are fun and easy to follow through the woods and around the pond. Pickup a trail map at the entrance kiosk or in the visitor center and follow the trail rules to spend several enjoyable hours on the grounds. A long boardwalk spans one section of the pond allowing for a good view of pond life below it. The trails are open from dawn to dusk. The building is open from Tuesday through Saturday 8:30 AM to 4:30 PM year around. From April through October, it is also open from 12:30 PM to 5:30 PM Sundays.

Note: Birthday parties can be scheduled at the center for $30 for up to 12 children. Nature hikes, games, activities and favors are provided for entertainment. Reservations are needed. Picnic tables are located on the grounds. A room is available to rent for indoor parties. Party treats are brought by parents.

*MICHAELS KIDS CLUB
Michaels The Arts and Crafts Store

Imagination Saturdays is a Saturday morning between 10 AM and noon stop by hands-on arts and crafts program for children ages five to twelve. All Michaels stores offer this activity. A new project is taught in the store's classroom each week. It could be a feathered mask, a mini clay pot, a windsock or key chain. Often the project has a holiday or seasonal theme like a love bug visor to wear on Valentine's Day or a snowman fridge magnet. A small activity fee of $2 per child includes all materials. Child size aprons for messy projects are offered. Dads and moms can participate. However, they need not stay in the room but can browse in the store during club time.

Stop by your nearest Michaels for a monthly flyer listing the craft projects. They are also displayed on the classroom wall.

Note: Craft parties can be arranged for birthdays, school groups, scouts and others. Contact the store's event coordinator or stop by your nearest store for a brochure and details. Their Play & Create! Craft Parties for Creative Kids brochure has a selection of projects that begin at $6 per child.

*MILL CITY MUSEUM
Minnesota Historical Society (MHS)
704 2nd St. S.
Minneapolis, 55401

612-341-7555 (infoline)
www.millcitymuseum.org

Did you know that from 1880 to 1930 Minneapolis was known as the "Flour Capital of the World." And the Washburn A Mill was the most technically advanced and largest in the world until replace by the Pillsbury Mill on the other side of the river.

Restored and operated by the MHS, the mill opened as a museum in 2003. Look for the Gold Medal Flour outdoor sign when going for a visit. The museum is located next door to it.

Today, there are many hands-on activities that children of ages six and older will find of interest and fun. There is the Water Lab, the Baking Lab and the Flour Tower Show, a must experience. The show is a 12 minute elevator ride that travels eight floors stopping at several for viewing reconstructed rooms depicting life in the mill when in operation. Recorded messages tell the Washburn mill's story throughout the ride.

The Charles H. Bell Ruin Courtyard is of interest as it shows remains of the mill's limestone walls now left open to the sky.

Finally be sure to climb the stairs or ride an elevator to the 9th floor indoor/outdoor observation deck. The view looking east over the Mississippi River is spectacular.

Museum admission is adults $8, seniors $6, children six to 17 $4 and five and under free. The museum hours are Tuesday through Saturday 10 AM to 5 PM except Thursday when open until 9 PM. Sunday hours are noon to 5 PM.

Note: Birthday party packages that include a scavenger hunt activity are available. Fees begin at $120 for up to 12 people with MHS members receiving a discount. For reservations and ways to customize a party, contact the museum scheduler at 612-341-7556.

MINNEAPOLIS INSTITUTE OF ARTS (MIA)
2400 3rd Ave. S.
Minneapolis, 55404

612-870-3131 (infoline)
1-888-642-2787
www.artsmia.org

One of the most enjoyable places for children to go for exploring the different art forms is the MIA. Presently the Exploring Art series has children visiting the museum galleries followed by a related art activity based on what was seen. Classes and programs are offered for children age four and older with tuition starting at $25 for members. Non-member fees are a few dollars more. For a listing of the youth classes and programs as well as registration materials and fee information, contact the MIA for a copy of their Youth Programs brochure. The MIA website has information on upcoming youth programs also.

Admission to the institute is free. However, some special exhibits may charge admission. The institute is open Tuesday through Saturday from 10 AM to 5 PM except on Thursday evenings when it is open until 9 PM. Sundays the institute is open from noon to 5 PM. It is closed on Mondays.

Group tours of ten or more children of kindergarten age and up are available with reservation needed at least four weeks prior to visit. A list of suggested tour topics is on MIA's website as well as a printable mailable tour request form. Tour information is also available by calling the tour office at 612-870-3140.

Note: One Sunday each month between 11 AM and 5 PM, MIA has a free Family Day art happening event. The dates and themes for these along with the planned activities are located by selecting the Events by Type option on MIA's website.

And be sure to check out the new Family Center on the first floor. It is for parents with children of infant age to seven when a break is needed.

MINNEAPOLIS PARK & RECREATION BOARD (MP&RB)
2117 W. River Rd.
Minneapolis, 55411

612-230-6400
www.minneapolisparks.com

Minneapolis has 50 excellent community and neighborhood centers. In 1989 MP&RB was named the winner of the National Gold Medal Award at the National Recreation & Park Association Congress. It is an award honoring excellence in park and recreational management. Programs, classes and recreational activities are planned for preschoolers throughout the year at each center. For elementary age children, arts & crafts classes, dance, active games and sports programs are scheduled for after school, Saturdays and on week days during the summer months at most centers. Neighborhood Naturalist Programs are offered at some of the centers. The programs have environmental educational themes and activities such as learning about squiggly and squirmy bugs, snakes and worms or using recycled materials to make nature art. Some of the classes have small fees for materials or instruction costs. Visit the website or ask at your nearest center for current and upcoming activities and special events.

The park board encourages residents with children to use the beaches, boat docks, fishing docks, picnic areas and hiking and biking trails. During the summer, swimming lessons are offered at some of the beaches, at the two new water parks and Webber Pool. During the winter months, there are ski lessons, snowboarding and snow tubing at Theodore Wirth, as well as skating rinks at many centers.

MINNEAPOLIS PUBLIC LIBRARY
300 Nicollet Mall
Minneapolis, 55401

612-630-6000
www.mpls.lib.mn.us

Children can check-out books, magazines, CDs, DVDs, videos, cassette tapes and talking books with a free library card. The card can be applied for when accompanied by a parent or guardian who has appropriate photo resident ID information for verification. Materials can be taken home for three weeks. A replacement cost is charged for a child's non-returned materials. A monthly brochure called EVENTS lists the many programs planned for each library during the month. It can be picked up at any one of the Minneapolis libraries.

Each library has a summer reading program with activities planned to encourage children and families to read together.

Note: The Downtown Library's Children's Library (612-630-6280) has an extensive language collection of children's books. There are many books in over 30 different languages including Vietnamese, Chinese, Somali, Oromo (East Africa), Hmong, Hindi, Russian and an especially large collection in Spanish. They recently added a collection of braille books with English text. Many of these are picture books.

As the hours vary from library to library, check with the library or visit the website before going to a library.

EAST LAKE: 2727 E. Lake St., 55406 (612-630-6550)

FRANKLIN: 1314 E. Franklin Ave., 55404 (612-630-6800)

HOSMER: 347 E. 36th St., 55408 (612-630-6950)

LINDEN HILLS: 2900 W. 43rd St., 55410 (612-630-6750)

MINNEAPOLIS (Downtown): 300 Nicollet Mall, 55401 (612-630-6000)

NOKOMIS: 5100 34th Ave. S., 55417 (612-630-6700)

NORTH REGIONAL: 1315 Lowry Ave. N., 55411 (612-630-6600)

NORTHEAST: 2200 Central Ave. N.E., 55418 (612-630-6900)

PIERRE BOTTINEAU: 55 Broadway St. N.E., 55413 (612-630-6890)

ROOSEVELT: 4026 28th Ave. S., 55406 (612-630-6590)

SOUTHEAST: 1222 S.E. 4th St., 55414 (612-630-6850)

SUMNER: 611 Van White Memorial Blvd., 55411
(612-630-6390)

WALKER: 2880 Hennepin Ave., 55408 (612-630-6650)

WASHBURN: 5244 Lyndale Ave. S., 55419 (612-630-6500)

WEBBER PARK: 4310 Webber Pkwy., 55412 (612-630-6640)

MINNEAPOLIS SCULPTURE GARDEN
1750 Hennepin Ave.
Vineland Place across from Walker Art Center at Lyndale &
Hennepin Aves.
Minneapolis, 55403

612-375-7609 (tour office infoline)
www.walkerart.org

The Minneapolis Sculpture Garden is located on 11 acres of land. On display are more than 40 sculptures divided among four 100-foot square plazas with walking paths defining the spaces. Favorites of families include the huge Spoonbridge and Cherry sculpture located in the gardens and the 65-foot tall Standing Glass Fish in the Cowles Conservatory. In the Judy and Kenneth Dayton Sculpture Plaza, children, with a boost up, can gently swing on the Arikidea sculpture's rope platform and climb through the Ordovician Pore. A free and very informative garden guide brochure is available in the conservatory. Pick one up. There are lots to see and talk about when visiting this unique and popular attraction.

The garden is open from 6 AM to midnight every day of the year. The conservatory hours are Tuesday, Wednesday, Saturday from 10 AM to 8 PM, Thursday and Friday 10 AM until 9 PM and Sunday from 11 AM to 5 PM.

Walk-in tours are offered on weekends at 1 PM May through September. Meet the tour guide in the Walker Art Center lobby. No reservations are needed. Call for information on scheduling a group tour.

Note: A backpack, called a WAC Pack, has games and activities for families to use in exploring the gardens. It can be checked out with paid admission at the Walker Art lobby desk.

MINNEHAHA DEPOT
Minnesota Transportation Museum (MTM)
Located in Minnehaha Park on Minnehaha Ave. near 49th St. E.
Minneapolis, 55417

651-228-0263 (infoline)
www.mtmuseum.org
www.mnhs.org/places/sites/md/index.html

This is one of the last Victorian-style railway stations left in Minnesota. It was built in the mid-1870s and is known as The Princess because of its delicate gingerbread architecture. Today the depot is open Sunday afternoons and holidays from 12:30 to 4:30 PM from Memorial Day through Labor Day and during the school year by reservation. Operated by MTM, additional information can be had by calling or visiting the websites.

MINNEHAHA FALLS & PARK
Minnehaha Pkwy. along the Mississippi River
Minneapolis, 55417

The falls was immortalized by Longfellow in his poem, *The Song of Hiawatha*, and is an enjoyable place to visit throughout the year. In the winter, the falls are frozen into fascinating patterns. In the summer, a flight of steps can be followed to a landing just below the falls. A statue of Hiawatha is located above the falls.

MINNESOTA AIR GUARD MUSEUM
ANG Base at Minneapolis & St. Paul International Airport
Hwys. 62 & 55
P.O. Box 11598
St. Paul, 55111

612-713-2523
www.mnangmuseum.org

The museum is located on the Minnesota Air National Guard base in the northeast corner of the airport near Ft. Snelling. Vintage aircraft, pictures, memorabilia and artifacts tell the story of the Minnesota's 109th Aero Squadron from its beginning in 1921 to the present. There are 15 aircraft on display in the airpark including the sleek A-12 Blackbird. Code named "oxcart 128" it is described as the highest and fastest flying airplane in the world. The oldest planes date back to the late 1930s. The museum is open mid-April through mid-September most Saturdays from 11 AM to 4 PM and Sundays from noon to 4 PM. Private tours at other times can be arranged. Call to book a tour.

All visitors must arrive by car. All adults must have a picture ID. Visit the website for current calendar of events. Donations are welcome.

*MINNESOTA CENTER FOR BOOK ARTS (MCBA)

1011 Washington Ave. So., Suite 100
Minneapolis, 55415

612-215-2520 (infoline)
www.mnbookarts.org

The center offers seasonal classes and events in papermaking, bookmaking and printing. They are designed for children ages two and up. A recent class created a holiday card using the center's paper pulp and molds with beads, ribbons, photographs, etc. brought from home. Classes are on Saturdays with special events on other days also. Some events are free, others have fees ranging from $24 to $36 with discounts for members and some are limited in size. Call for a seasonal brochure or visit the website for the current offerings.

Youth workshops and field trips are available at MCBA, too. They are of one to three hours long and include an introduction to the world of book arts and a hands-on activity. This could include making a book, making paper or printing a page. Groups up to 100 can be accommodated. Reservations are required. A fee of $5 to $20 per person is charged. The fee depends on the selected project. Contact the Youth Workshops Program coordinator at 612-215-2529 for arrangements.

*MINNESOTA DEPARTMENT OF NATURAL RESOURCES (DNR)
DNR Information Center
500 Lafayette Rd.
St. Paul, 55155

651-296-6157
1-888-646-6367
www.dnr.state.mn.us

An one year park permit for unlimited visits to all 72 Minnesota state parks and recreation areas can be purchased for $25. The vehicle permit sticker can be purchased at all state parks, at the DNR Information Center and on the website.

Note: The DNR website is one of the best for ease of use yet discovered. Choices of divisions, regional offices, related pages, events, newsroom, etc., as well as a search box are clear and helpful. It even gives the current weather conditions in St. Paul with option to change city location.

*MINNESOTA HISTORY CENTER (MHC)
Minnesota Historical Society (MHS)
345 Kellogg Blvd. W.
St. Paul, 55102

651-259-3000
1-800-657-3773
www.mnhs.org/historycenter

Did you know that Minnesota gets its name from the Dakota Indian word "minisota" which means sky-tinted waters. Did you know that Minnesota waters flow in three directions: north to Canada's Hudson Bay, east to the Atlantic Ocean and south to the Gulf of Mexico and that no water flows into the state.

With the mission of the Society to collect, preserve, interpret and exhibit Minnesota history, these and other interesting history facts can be discovered when visiting the History Center.

In answer to "How did SooLine boxcar #137356 get in the building?" watch the short video in the Going Places exhibit and find out. "Is the boxcar ready to roll?" You decide by checking for defects. In the Sounds Good to Me! exhibit, memories of the Prom Ballroom can be shared by the older with the younger. At Home Place, younger children can be active by packing the oxcart with pretend fur pelts and meat. Other exhibits are Weather Permitting and Open House: If These Walls Could Talk.

Special family events are occasionally held usually on a weekend afternoon throughout the year. At each event a hands-on, take-home activity program formerly called History Hi-Jinx is planned for children and families. The activity is history related to the theme of the event so they learn about Minnesota history. So far children have learned a game for collecting their family's stories plus a treasure chest to keep them in and have built miniature shimmering ice palaces among many other fun projects. The activity has no added fee, the project's materials are provided and no reservation is needed.

History Matters, the MHS's bimonthly publication, contains events announcements and articles at all their sites including MHC's. Pick up a copy at your next visit. Or become a member and have it mailed to you. Members also can visit free of charge most MHS sites.

The center is open Tuesday through Saturday from 10 AM to 5 PM except on Tuesday evening when it is open until 8 PM. Sunday the center is open from noon until 5 PM. Admission is $8 for adults, $6 for seniors and college students, $4 for children six to 17. Library admission is free. Parking is $1.50 to $7 depending on length of stay.

Note: The Education Department (651-296-1696) **www.mnhs.org/ fieldtrips** offers Student Field Trips programs for prekindergarten age children and older. Call for the History Field Trips brochure or visit the website for more information. Costs are $2 to $6 per person. To schedule a field trip program call 651-297-7258.

MINNESOTA STATE CAPITOL BUILDING TOUR
Minnesota Historical Society (MHS)
75 Rev. Dr. Martin Luther King Jr. Blvd.
At Aurora & Park Ave.
St. Paul, 55155

651-296-2881 (infoline)
www.mnhs.org/places/sites/msc
www.leg.state.mn.us/leg/youth

The capitol is located just a few blocks north of downtown St. Paul in the Capitol Complex area. Architect Cass Gilbert designed our marble dome to be similar to that of the capitol's dome in Washington, D.C. Opened in 1905, the State Capitol houses the chambers for the two branches of State Legislature, the Governor's office and the Supreme Court. The second website above has Just for Fun activities for children located at the Kids tab.

On a tour, one hears about the capitol's history, art and architecture, visits the government chambers and weather allowing, can walk to the capitol's roof to see the golden horses.

Regularly scheduled guided tours lasting about 45 minutes leave hourly from 9 AM to 3 PM Monday through Friday and from 10 AM to 2 PM on Saturdays and at 1, 2, 3 PM on Sundays.

Educational group tours of ten or more for preschool children and older are asked to make reservations at least two weeks in advance by calling 651-296-2881. A fee of $2 to $4 per person is charged for this tour.

Special events are held at the capitol throughout the year. These have admission fees of $7 adults and $4 seniors and children six to 17.

Note: On a family visit, purchase the Art Treasures in the Minnesota State Capitol brochure for $2. Use it for a scavenger hunt activity. Record finding the objects [there's the griffin and Colonel Colvill's statue and ten others], with a gold sticker star. Don't forget to collect the special seal reward for finding all of them at the Information Deck.

MINNESOTA VALLEY NATIONAL WILDLIFE REFUGE
3815 American Blvd. E.
Bloomington, 55425

952-854-5900
www.fws.gov/midwest/minnesotavalley

Described as one of the best-kept secrets in the Twin Cities, this wildlife center needs to be discovered. Open 9 AM to 5 PM Tuesday through Sunday. Closed on Mondays and holidays. The interpretive and education center was built for the U.S. Fish and Wildlife Service in 1990. It has a hiking trail that leads to a marsh in the valley. A multi-level exhibition hall has many hands-on exhibits for children to try. Through visiting the exhibits, one can learn how the river valley was formed and all about the refuge's grasslands and marshlands and river channel.

The center now offers free educational programs for children of kindergarten age and older. Visit the website or call for information on these.

*MINNETONKA CENTER FOR THE ARTS (MCA)
2240 North Shore Dr.
Wayzata, 55391

952-473-7361 (infoline)
www.minnetonkaarts.org/home.html

During the school year, Saturdays are special days for children at the center with additional classes now also offered Tuesday evenings. Workshops and classes in drawing, paints, clay, collage and sculpting are offered for children ages five and up. Member fees for children's classes begin at $47 and workshop fees begin at $40. There are additional materials fee. Non-members fees are $5 to $10 more. A catalog with all the workshop and class offerings can be requested by contacting them. The website also contains current information on classes and events at the center.

The center hours are Monday through Thursday 9 AM to 9:30 PM and Friday and Saturday 9 AM to 5 PM. Summer Saturday hours are 9 AM to 1 PM.

Note: MCA Summer Arts Camp is designed to allow children ages five to 12 years old to explore various media including drawing, jewelry, clay and fabric art. There is much flexibility in session lengths to allow for all the other activities going on during the summer. Half-day sessions start at $23 for non-members and $20 for members. Contact the center for all the details.

*NORTHERN CLAY CENTER (NCC)
2424 Franklin Ave. E.
Minneapolis, 55406

612-339-8007 (infoline)
www.northernclaycenter.org

Hands-on clay events for ages six and older can be arranged with three weeks advance notice required. Children will make a clay project and glaze it. The item is fired and ready for pick up to take home a few weeks later. Possible projects include a mask, vase, treasure box and of course, the always can't have enough, mug. The two hour event is $150 for up to ten people. This is a good birthday party event.

The NCC offers a free guided tour with advance notice. Also a wheel demonstration is available for $35. During the demo, an artist creates pots on the potter's wheel.

The NCC has Clay for Kids classes for ages nine and up beginning at $145 and Clay for Families one day events for age six and up for $40 for two people.

The center is open Tuesday through Saturday from 10 AM to 6 PM and Sunday from noon to 4 PM. Closed Mondays. Contact the center to request a clay events brochure and class listing newsletter or visit the website. Parking is convenient in lot adjacent to building.

*OMNITHEATER
Located in the Science Museum of Minnesota
120 W. Kellogg Blvd.
St. Paul, 55102

651-221-9444 (infoline)
www.smm.org

The William L. McKnight-3M Omnitheater is one of the most popular attractions in the Twin Cities. The world's largest film projector, the Omnimax, projects 70 mm film onto a rotating dome giving the viewer the feeling of being in the middle of the projected action. This could be hang gliding over the surf of the Big Sur or riding in a hot air balloon over a New England church steeple or careening down a snowy trail in northern Minnesota on a snowmobile. The showtimes are on the hour beginning at 10 AM until 9 PM depending on the day of the week and season of the year. Each show lasts about one hour.

As the Omni is so popular, especially on Sunday afternoons, arrive early to purchase tickets. They are $7.50 for adults and $5.50 for seniors and children four to 12. Reservations can be made for an additional $2 per ticket by calling 651-221-9444 at least two hours in advance. For current show information and times, visit the website or call the infoline.

Note: School groups can arrange weekday morning ShowTimes and receive special rates by contacting the Omni a month in advance of the planned visit.

*ORCHESTRA HALL
The Minnesota Orchestra
1111 Nicollet Mall
Minneapolis, 55403

5642-5642-5642 (infoline)
612-371-5656
www.minnesotaorchestra.org/aim

The Minnesota Orchestra presents each year a subscription series of concerts called Adventures in Music for Families. Recommended for children ages eleven and under, the performances are at 2 PM and 4 PM on four Sunday afternoons usually scheduled between November and March. This is a wonderful way for families to explore music together. Series ticket prices start at $29 and up for children and $48 and up for adults. Single performance ticket prices range from $12 to $35. For ticket and current program information on the series, contact the orchestra to request a brochure or visit the website.

Young People's Concerts is another musical experience. These concerts are designed for school children of elementary age and older, scheduled on weekdays at 10 AM and 11:35 AM and usually are about one hour long. Each school year, a series of unique programs are planned. Examples of programs have included Swinging Nutcracker, Beethoven's Fifth and At the Movies with the Minnesota Orchestra. Schools and educational groups can request a brochure and reservation information through contacting 612-371-5671 or visiting the website. Group prices are $5 and $ 6 per ticket. Reservations begin in April for the following school year.

Another extremely popular program is the WAMSO Kinder Konzerts. These are designed for children four and five years old who are in preschools and nursery schools or come with an adult. The programs are short and fun. They are held on 12 different weekday mornings throughout the school year at 9:20 AM and 11 AM. To request a brochure describing the details, contact WAMSO office at 612-371-5654 or visit their website **www.wamso.org**

*ORDWAY CENTER FOR THE PERFORMING ARTS
Education and Community Engagement at Ordway
345 Washington St.
St. Paul, 55102

651-282-3115 (infoline)
www.ordway.org

The Ordway's education staff plans a series of 15 performing arts programs for young people each school year. At 10:30 AM and 12:45 PM, the series includes multi-cultural dance and music performances. Children of elementary grade and older may attend. Tickets range from $3 to $6 per person per program. Start planning for these programs in late summer as they are very popular and reservations made well in advance are a must.

*PAVEK MUSEUM OF BROADCASTING
3515 Raleigh Ave.
St. Louis Park, 55416

952-926-8198
www.museumofbroadcasting.com

This museum's beginnings date back to 1919 when Joseph R. Pavek built a crystal receiving set and a Model T Ford spark coil transmitter. Today, the museum houses thousands of radio sets, transmitters and broadcasting station equipment as well as a library of books on electricity, magnetism and other subjects related to the development of the radio.

The museum is open to the public year around Tuesday through Friday 10 AM to 6 PM and Saturdays from 9 AM to 5 PM. It is closed Sunday and Monday. Call to arrange for special tours or large group visits. The website has information on upcoming events, educational opportunities and a location map. Admission is $6 for adults and $5 for students and seniors. It is suggested that children in grades four and above will find the museum's displays of most interest.

If you enjoyed the Bakken Museum, you will want to visit this one too.

PINE TREE APPLE ORCHARD
450 Apple Orchard Rd.
White Bear Lake, 55110

651-429-7202 (infoline)
www.pinetreeappleorchard.com

In September and October, a guided tour of the orchards at Pine Tree may be arranged through reservations made in advance. During busy times when guided tours are not possible, groups can go on self-guided tours and see where apple sorting, the cider press operations, etc. are located. Judging from the many thank you letters written by children and posted on a wall in the salesroom, the touring is fun. We enjoy going to the special weekend events held in the fall which have included in past years wagon rides, pick your own pumpkin and a corn maze. Open from June through February, a trip to this orchard to pick your own strawberries beginning in mid-June and to buy apples, cider, pie or apple donuts beginning in August has always been an enjoyable experience for our family.

Located off E. Hwy. 96 in a woodsy setting, getting to this orchard is part of the fun. Watch carefully for their signs! As hours very with the season, you are advised to call or visit the website before going.

*THE PLANETARIUM
At the top of the new Minneapolis Public Library Building
300 Nicollet Mall
Minneapolis, 55401

612-630-6150 (infoline)
www.mplanetarium.org

The planetarium features programs on astronomy and the space sciences. Currently closed, the proposed planetarium with new space discovery center plans to reopen in 2008 or 2009. Visit the website for updates.

Three newly discovered sites that can be visited for night star gazing, star shows, and sky education programs:

*Como Planetarium in Como Elemenatry School, 780 W. Wheelock Pky., St. Paul, 55117, 651-293-5398 (infoline)
www.planetarium.spps.org
Public visits selected Thursdays and school field trips. Admission $4 per person.

Eisenhower Observatory in Eisenhower Community Center, 1001 Hwy. 7, Hopkins, 55305, 952-988-4077 **www.hopkins.k12.mn.us**
Public visits and school field trips. No fee but donations accepted.

*Onan Observatory in Baylor Regional Park, 10775 Cty. Rd. 33, Norwood/Young America, 55397, 952-467-2426 (infoline)
www.mnastro.org/onan
Free monthly public star gazing events April through November weather permitting. Park entry requires daily fee or annual pass.

Let the Stars Shine for You!

POLICE STATIONS
Most police stations welcome visits by young children. During a visit, police officers like to emphasize their role in helping people in the community. The officers like to talk to children about the importance of safety when riding a bicycle and walking in the street. In Minneapolis, contact the Commander of one of the five precinct stations to arrange a visit: 612-673-5701 for Precinct 1, 612-673-5702 for Precinct 2, 612-673-5703 for Precinct 3, 612-673-5704 for Precinct 4 or 612-673-5705 for Precinct 5 to arrange a community group tour. It is best to call between the hours of 8 AM and 4 PM.

In St. Paul, police officer visits can be arranged by requesting in writing the date, time, place for the visit, ages of the children and topics of interest to be covered. The request should be addressed to the Chief of Police,

367 Grove St., St. Paul, 55101. Additional questions can be answered by calling 651-266-5639 weekdays.

Most other communities when contacted will help arrange a visit to their building. Some police departments will arrange school visits also.

Note: 5TH PRECINCT STATION, 3101 Nicollet Ave. S., Minneapolis, 55408 (612-673-5705) has on exhibit in display cases a small collections of weapons and photographs. There is no longer a need to contact the station to make arrangements for a visit. Just drop by to see them.

RAMSEY COUNTY HISTORICAL SOCIETY (RCHS)
323 Landmark Center
75 W. 5th St.
St. Paul, 55102

651-222-0701
www.rchs.com

"Exploring history close to home" is the theme of RCHS. One of its main attractions is the Gibbs Museum, the oldest remaining farmhouse in Ramsey County, where special programs and events are held throughout the year for families and children's groups. Discover more information about the museum in the G's, its alphabetical location. To receive a seasonal calendar of all the RCHS events, contact the society weekdays during the office hours of 9 AM to 5 PM or visit their website to locate their History News and Notes Online Newsletter.

RAMSEY COUNTY LIBRARY
Administrative Offices
4570 Victoria St.
Shoreview, 55126

651-486-2200
www.rclreads.org

Children under 18 years of age can receive a library card with a parent or guardian's assistance of current picture and address identification. There are no age restrictions. Books, magazines, DVDs, videocassettes, audio books and CDs can be checked out. Most materials are loaned for three weeks. DVDs and videocassettes are one week loans. Overdue childrens items are 10 cents per day per item except for DVDs and videocassettes that are $1 per day.

Storytimes are held frequently for toddlers and preschool age children at all libraries. Maplewood and Roseville libraries have Lapsit, a program for babies as young as six months. Summer reading programs are scheduled at all libraries.

As the hours vary from library to library, contact the nearest one for these. And then visit to pickup a Library Guide brochure and a copy of their seasonal publication, Explore Your Guide to News & Events. The website contains much of this information as well.

ARDEN HILLS: 1941 W. Cty. Rd. E2, 55112 (651-628-6831)

MAPLEWOOD: 1670 Beam Ave., 55109 (651-704-2033)

MOUNDS VIEW: 2576 Cty. Rd. 10, 55112 (651-717-3272)

NORTH ST. PAUL: 2290 N. 1st St., 55109 (651-747-2700)

ROSEVILLE: 2180 N. Hamline Ave., 55113 (651-628-6803)

SHOREVIEW: 4570 N. Victoria St., 55126 (651-486-2300)

WHITE BEAR LAKE: 4698 Clark Ave., 55110 (651-407-5302)

RAMSEY COUNTY PARKS & RECREATION DEPT.
2015 N. Van Dyke St.
Maplewood, 55109

651-748-2500
www.co.ramsey.mn.us/parks

The parks and recreation areas in Ramsey County are used for many children's activities. Swimming, boating, hiking, fishing, picnicking and cross-country skiing are available in most of the parks. Skating instruction is offered at several ice arenas including the Charles M. Schulz-Highland Ice Arena. For more information on the use of the parks and recreation areas and skating instruction, call or write the department or visit the website and subscribe to Announcements and News delivered via e-mail. The office hours are 8 AM to 4:30 PM Monday through Friday.

Note: Battle Creek WATERWORKS Family Aquatic Center is an outdoor water park open from early June through mid-August from late mornings to early evenings. It is located at 2401 Upper Afton Rd. in Battle Creek Regional Park, Maplewood. Admission is $5.50 for adults and children. Visit the website **www.co.ramsey.mn.us/parts/ parks/waterworks.asp** or call for current seasonal information.

*THE RAPTOR CENTER (TRC)
University of Minnesota
St. Paul Campus
1920 Fitch Ave.
St. Paul, 55108

612-624-4745 (infoline)
www.theraptorcenter.org

TRC has an international reputation for helping eagles and other birds of prey recover from injuries. Attend Raptors of Minnesota, a regularly scheduled program, for individuals, families and small groups on Saturday and Sunday at 1 PM to learn more about the good care going on here. Call 612-624-9753 to preregister. We saw Zepher, an American Kestrel, on our visit. He was described as a human imprint, a bird raised as a pet and thus unable to be set free as he didn't know how to hunt for food. Also on the tour were displays showing the steps from a bird's admission to release. A surgery table and medical tools are part of the exhibit. There were also drawers containing bird wings, eggs and exercise equipment. The tour ends with a walk through the outdoor courtyard where there are more than twenty educational raptors.

Programs for schools, scout and other groups of twelve and up to 90 can be arranged. Contact 612-624-2756 to make a reservation. The presentations are about one hour in length and are led by very knowledgeable volunteers.

Admission for programs and presentations are $7.50 adult and $5 student and senior citizen. The center hours are Tuesday through Friday 10 AM to 4 PM and Saturday and Sunday noon to 4 PM.

Community Off-Site programs are available, too. Call 612-624-2756 or visit the website for the details including fees for these programs.

Note: Spring and Fall Raptor Release events are held with the main activity at each the release of recovered birds. The spring release is held at an East Metro park location and the fall release is held in a West Metro park. Call or visit the website for the next release date and its location..

THE RED BALLOON BOOKSHOP
Children's Books, Etc.
891 Grand Ave.
St. Paul, 55105

651-224-8320
1-888-224-8320
www.redballoonbookshop.com

Regularly scheduled Tuesday mornings storytimes are 10:15 for babies and 11 for toddlers with Wednesday morning at 10:30 now for preschoolers. Held in a corner of the bookshop, these are an excellent opportunity to introduce children to the love for reading. Saturday at 10:30 AM is for events with a different program each time. Other events for children and families are offered throughout the year. All have connections to reading and books. A newsletter of the events is available in the bookshop or if requested, they will mail you one. The bookshop is open seven days a week.

*ST. PAUL CHAMBER ORCHESTRA (SPCO)
The Hamm Building 3rd Floor
408 St. Peter St.
St. Paul, 55102

651-292-3248
www.thespco.org

The SPCO performs special concerts for young people each orchestra season. The Family Series Concerts is a series of four concerts particularly suited for children ages six to twelve. Children have opportunities to talk to the conductor and musicians at each performance. Themes for concerts have included Our Musical Earth and Bach Bluegrass and Bugs. For series ticket information, contact SPCO at 651-291-1144 or visit the website. Series tickets are $26 to $58. Individual concert tickets are $8 to $18.

Concerts are held Saturday mornings at the Ordway Center for the Performing Arts in St. Paul. As the concert formats vary from season to season, information on the SPCO current season's programs can be had through calling or website.

Note: Offered two times a year, Start the Music is an event for families with young children ages three to six. One Saturday morning each fall and spring, SPCO plans a new program to introduce children to a classical music experience through interacting with the music, the musicians and their instruments. Tickets are $8.

ST. PAUL PARKS & RECREATION DEPT.
300 City Hall Annex
25 W. 4th St.
St. Paul, 55102

651-266-6400 (infoline)
www.stpaul.gov/depts/parks

St. Paul has 41 recreation centers and recommends contacting the closest one in your community for a schedule of its planned activities. Another option is to call their brochure request line (651-266-6463) to receive information through the mail. Como Park offers downhill ski lessons for children ages four and older. Como Park also has cross-country skiing lessons and rentals. Registration with fees for instruction are required. Swimming programs are offered during the summer at the outdoor pools and Phalen beach. Fees are charged for swim lessons. All pools have open swim with admission fee of $4 adults, $3.50 seniors and $2.50 for children ages 17 and under. Discounted swim passes are also available.

Note: Great River Water Park (formerly Oxford Pool) has re-opened at 270 N. Lexington Parkway (651-642-0650). Following extensive renovation, the large kiddie pool features a wooden raft with sprayers and slides. Open swim times and the always friendly, watchful lifeguards have returned.

ST. PAUL PUBLIC LIBRARY
Central Library
90 W. 4th St.
St. Paul, 55102

651-266-7000 (infoline)
www.sppl.org

Children's books and most other library materials can be borrowed for three weeks with a library card. Children of any age can have a card. A parent, guardian or teacher can assist the very young child in obtaining his or her card. The Central Library has a wonderful Youth Services Room (651-266-7034). They and many other libraries have children's programs during the school year. All libraries have storytimes and summer reading programs. Pamphlets and brochures identifying the many reading activities including lists of recommended books are available in all the libraries. As the libraries have varying hours, check with the library before a visit. Or better still pick up the Visit Your Library brochure available at every library or visit the website as each has a map of all locations with their hours open.

Note: At the Central Library, Saturday Live with performers like puppeteers, magicians and musicians present a free program for families with children of all ages at 11:15 AM.

ARLINGTON HILLS: 1105 Greenbrier St., 55106 (651-793-3930)

CENTRAL: 90 W. 4th St., 55102 (651-266-7000)

DAYTON'S BLUFF: 645 E. 7th St., 55106 (651-793-1699)

HAMLINE MIDWAY: 1558 W. Minnehaha, 55104 (651-642-0293)

HAYDEN HEIGHTS: 1456 White Bear Ave., 55106 (651-793-3934)

HIGHLAND PARK: 1974 Ford Pky., 55116 (651-695-3700)

MERRIAM PARK: 1831 Marshall Ave., 55104 (651-642-0385)

RICE STREET: 1011 Rice St., 55117 (651-558-2223)

RIVERVIEW: 1 E. George St., 55107 (651-292-6626)

RONDO COMMUNITY OUTREACH: 461 No. Dale St., 55104
(651-642-0359)

ST. ANTHONY PARK: 2245 Como Ave., 55108 (651-642-0411)

SKYWAY: 56 E. 6 St. #203, 55101 (651-292-7141)

SUN RAY: 2105 Wilson, 55119 (651-501-6300)

WEST SEVENTH: 265 Oneida St., 55102 (651-298-5516)

St. Paul Public operates a Bookmobile that visits many city locations on a bi-weekly schedule. For information on these locations and scheduled times, contact the Bookmobile office at 651-642-0379 or visit the website.

ST. PAUL REGIONAL WATER SERVICES (SPRWS)
McCarron Treatment Plant
1900 Rice St. N.
Maplewood, 55113

651-266-6350
www.ci.stpaul.mn.us/water

Guided tours for school groups of sixth grade age and up can be arranged. During the tour, students see and are told about the processing of our surface water as it flows through the treating, filtering and pumping steps. It is best to schedule the visit at a time when class is studying water science.

Note: Popular public tours are offered in May during the SPRWS's Open House.

*ST. PAUL SAINTS BASEBALL TEAM
Midway Stadium
1771 Energy Park Dr.
St. Paul, 55108

651-644-6659
www.saintsbaseball.com

The St. Paul Saints baseball team plays in an outdoor stadium to fans of all ages. They are in the American Association League with teams from Sioux City IA, Sioux Falls SD, Lincoln NE, Fort Worth TX and others. The season begins in early May and ends in early September. Most games are at 7:05 PM except on Sunday when most start at 1:05 PM. Tickets cost from $4 to $12.

The Saints organization provides more than a ballgame to attendees. The game might be followed by all-star wrestling, fireworks and on-field autograph sessions. Between innings, a wedding could take place as it did one of the evenings we attended. Promotional activities include giveaways of baseball cards, bats and logo balls. And don't forget to wave at the trains. If lucky, you might catch one tooting their horn. All of the events are fun and planned with families in mind.

Note: Saints Kids Club is new and free. Join and receive a monthly E-Newsletter, five free Sunday home games based on availability, an autographed Mudonna baseball card and more. To sign up, call or through their website entering the password "pigpen."

*SCIENCE MUSEUM OF MINNESOTA (SMM)
120 W. Kellogg Blvd.
St. Paul, 55102

651-221-9444
www.smm.org

Think of our Science Museum of Minnesota as an upside down building. The main entrance on Kellogg Blvd. is the Lobby or Level 5. Level 6, Omni Theater, is up and Levels 4 through 1 are down.

Pick up a Visitor's Guide & Map. It identifies the permanent exhibits on each level and major attractions showing during your visit. Look for a kiosk located near the stairways. Daily Science Live programs and demonstration events are listed here.

In a quest to find Iggy, the steel nail-scaled iguana, who greeted visitors at the entrance to the old SMM on Wabasha and Exchange, we wandered down to Level 2 where we found him now welcoming visitors outside the Education entrance on Eagle and Chestnut. Children still cannot climb on him, but that's still O.K. because the new museum just like the old science museum encourages children to interact with most of the exhibits and ask lots of questions.

On Level 3 is another favorite, the Dinosaur and Fossil Gallery. Push a button to highlight the scar on the 82-foot-long triceratops dinosaur and read how the scar is thought to have come about!

The weekend of a new show or exhibit opening special hands on activities for children are planned in the Lobby entrance. For the Wolves opening, a child could trace his or her hand and then compare it to the size of a gray wolf's paw.

The 3-D Digital Cinema Show is a new feature. Viewers put on special 3-D glasses to see the 3-D images and hi-tech laser graphics. The educational themed shows change throughout the year. Reservations for the show can be made in advance. Tickets are $3 per person.

As so many varied learning experiences and activities for children on all levels and for all ages are offered, it is best to connect with SMM via calling or on the website for schedules of tours, events, attractions, classes, school and group programs.

The museum hours are Monday through Wednesday 9:30 AM to 5 PM,

Thursday through Saturday 9:30 AM to 9 PM and Sunday noon to 5 PM. It is still best to check on hours before going though as they are closed some holidays during the year. Admission is $9.50 for adults and $6.50 for seniors and children four to twelve. Memberships are available which reduce admissions and class fees. Call 651-221-9409 for membership information.

Note: Camp Wabasha is a summer arts day camp sponsored jointly by the museum and the Minnesota Museum of American Art. It offers young people a week of fun and adventure in the city. Art and science are included in each day's activities. Camp is for children age six through twelve. Tuition for the week is $120.

*SIBLEY HOUSE HISTORICAL SITE
Minnesota Historical Society (MHS)
1357 Sibley Memorial Hwy. near State Hwy. 55
Mendota, 55150

651-452-1596
www.mnhs.org

This is the home of the first governor of Minnesota. The house was recently refurbished in the period of the late 1830s to late 1850s. Built in 1836 for Henry Hastings Sibley, who was also a prominent fur trader and military leader, the house was the center of pioneer life. The Faribault House, located on the Sibley site, can be visited, too. It also has been restored and houses a fine collection of North American artifacts including pipes, beadwork and clothing items. On the southeast corner of the Sibley property is the Hypolite du Puis House reception center. Here special events are held.

The Sibley House is open daily Friday through Monday from Memorial Day through Labor Day from 10 AM to 4 PM except Sunday when it opens at 12:30 PM. In May through October, it is open on weekends only. Admission is $5 for adults, $4 for seniors and $3 for children ages six through 17. Children under six are admitted free. Admission includes visits to the Sibley and Faribault Houses as well as the Sibley Cold Store, a restored fur trading post also on the grounds. Tours are offered with the last one beginning at 3:45 PM.

During the winter and spring months, group and educational tours can be arranged.

Note: Special weekend events and programs are offered throughout the year. Children's Day includes playing games and doing activities popular during the mid-19th century. Fur Trade Encampment involves activities in the Cold Store. Call to inquire or visit the website about upcoming ones.

*SIERRA CLUB NORTH STAR CHAPTER
2327 E. Franklin Ave. Suite 1
Minneapolis, 55406

612-659-9124
www.northstar.sierraclub.org

The Sierra Club North Star Chapter has many outings some of which families would enjoy. Outing leaders are available to answer questions about the skill levels needed to participate in the activities. Families interested in more information should contact the club office or visit the website and click on Outings & Events.

The club published the North Star Journal newsletter with paper copies mailed to members. It is also available on the website.

*SPRINGBROOK NATURE CENTER
Fridley Recreation & Natural Resources Dept.
100 85th Ave. N.
Fridley, 55432

763-572-3588
www.springbrooknaturecenter.org

Springbrook Nature Center is located on 127 acres of park land only a half mile west of Northtown Mall on County Rd. 132. The Interpretive Center houses many exhibits and is the center from which many of their environmental and outdoor education programs originate. The center is open everyday of the year from 9 AM to 5 PM. The three miles of hiking trails are open from 5 AM to 10 PM daily.

A seasonal newsletter listing the special events and programs is available. Stop by or call the center or visit the website for it. The Spring Fling and Pumpkin Night in the Park are popular events. Scout programs and birthday parties are also. Many activities are free. Fees for programs, like Fun Hour for Young Children, start at $1.

*STAGES THEATRE COMPANY
Hopkins Center for the Arts
1111 Mainstreet
Hopkins, 55343

952-979-1111 (infoline)
www.stagestheatre.org

Children age four and up will enjoy the plays put on by this theatre company with the motto, Our World Is Magical. Six plays are presented throughout the season. Plays have included CindeEdna and Charlotte's Web. Admission is $14 for adults and $11 for seniors and children with group rates available. The plays are performed Wednesdays through Sundays and an occasional Monday.

In cooperation with Hopkins School District Community Education, many workshops and classes in acting are offered. Children as young as four can participate. Tuition begins at $50 with scholarships available.

*STEAMBOAT MINNEHAHA
Museum of Lake Minnetonka (MLM)
P.O. Box 178
Excelsior, 55331

952-474-2115
www.steamboatminnehaha.org

Steamboats provided Twin Citians with transportation across Lake Minnetonka from 1906 to 1926. The Minnehaha, scuttled in 1926, was raised from the lake in 1980 and completely restored by 1996.

Today, from late May through early October on Saturdays, Sundays and holidays, the Minnehaha provides rides once again on Lake Minnetonka. The trips are over two hours long and depart from either Wayzata or Excelsior. Fares are $12 to $15 for adults and $10 to $12 for seniors and children ages two to 12. Children have been known to be invited to steer the boat. For location directions, schedules and reservation information call or visit the website.

Note: A shorter, one hour cruise is now offered that may be just right for the family with younger children.

*STEPPINGSTONE THEATRE
55 Victoria St. N.
St. Paul, 55104

651-225-9265
www.steppingstonetheatre.org

The theater strives to help develop self-esteem, confidence, leadership skills and creativity in children through learning performance arts. It also has the goal of educating its audience through the kinds of plays it performs each season.

The performers are children of ages eight to 18. They have been selected from many diverse cultural backgrounds through open auditions. The plays are held year around in the F. K. Weyerhaeuser Auditorium located in Landmark Center and are varied in kind. They have included a musical featuring African-American dance, the Story of Hope, a mixed race child and their traditional holiday show, The Best Christmas Pageant Ever. Tickets are $9 with group discounts available. Performances are daily except Mondays. Call or visit the website for current performance information.

Note: School groups are encouraged to attend the plays. Request study guides when making reservations. The guides help prepare for what will be seen and then talked about after the performance.

*JOHN H. STEVENS HOUSE MUSEUM
4901 Minnehaha Ave. S.
Minneapolis, 55417

612-722-2220
www.johnhstevenshouse.org

Located in Minnehaha Falls Park, the Stevens house, the little white house, not the large yellow one, is the first permanent settler's home west of the Mississippi River and within the original city of Minneapolis. It is now restored to its original 1849-1850 appearance by the Junior League of Minneapolis and the Minneapolis Park & Recreation Board. Today, it is interpretive museum. Visitors will learn that it was also the first school house when the parlor became a classroom.

Weekdays, children in grade three and up in group tours can experience educational activities planned for them through advance reservations. The hours for other visitors are 1 PM to 5 PM Saturday, Sunday and holidays from Memorial Day through Labor Day. However, it is still best to contact the Stevens house when planning to visit. Admission is $2 for adults and $1 for ages 17 and under. Other tour groups should contact the tour coordinator for arrangements and special rates at other times.

Note: Monthly summer events are held on the lawn outside the house. These are free to the public. Visit the website for dates and the special activities planned on these days.

STORYTIMES

Most libraries and many bookstores in the Twin Cities have regularly scheduled storytime programs for children. Besides Saturdays, programs may be held after school for the older child, weekdays for the preschool and toddler ages and even evenings for children who can't attend during the day. Besides introducing books and other reading related activities, the librarians and storytellers like to present reading as a joyful, magical time. Contact the nearest library or ask at a children's bookstore about days and times.

TAMARACK NATURE CENTER
Ramsey County Parks & Recreation Dept.
Bald Eagle & Otter Lakes Regional Park
5287 Otter Lake Rd.
White Bear Lake, 55110

651-407-5350
www.co.ramsey.mn.us/parks/tamarack

This 320-acre preserve in White Bear Township has naturalists who will lead groups on hiking tours of the 3.5 miles of trails. Nature classes on subjects such as pond life, bird banding and animal tracking are offered to the public. Fees for programs range from free to $8. Schools and community groups can arrange for programs such as apple cider making and migration mysteries through advance arrangements. Day camps are offered in summer with fees ranging from $25 to $145.

The hiking trails are open a half hour before sunrise to a half hour after sunset. A naturalist is at the nature center from 8 AM to 4:30 PM Monday through Friday, 9 AM to 5 PM Saturday and noon to 5 PM on Sunday.

Note: Birthday parties can be held at the center with choices beginning at $60. Reservations in advance are necessary. For all the details, contact the center or visit the website.

*THOMAS C. SAVAGE VISITOR CENTER
101 Snelling Lake Rd. at State Hwy. 5 & Post Rd.
St. Paul, 55111

612-725-2724
www.dnr.state.mn.us/parks

Located within Fort Snelling State Park, the center offers programs throughout the year for families, groups and individuals interested in nature studies. One of the programs is the Annual Bluebird Recovery Workshop that includes a film, discussion on how to get started and information on bluebird houses. A schedule of their programs can be requested. The center is open to the public every day 9 AM to 4 PM. School and other groups by appointment can arrange for a group program at the center. An admission is charged for each vehicle entry onto the State Park grounds but not for the center's programs or visits. The daily park entry fee is $7 per vehicle. An annual pass for all Minnesota state parks is $25.

*THREE RIVERS PARK DISTRICT
Park District Headquarters
3000 Xenium Lane N.
Plymouth, 55441

763-559-9000 (infoline)
www.threeriversparkdistrict.org

Formerly known as Hennepin Parks, Three Rivers Park still offers many outdoor activities for families.

Explore the world of squirrels or observe birds preparing to hurry south for the winter or follow animal tracks on snowshoes. Depending on the time of the year, children can participate in these programs and many others. For a copy of Discoveries, the park publication listing the activities and programs planned for each season of the year, call 763-559-6708. Programs requiring reservations are made by calling 763-559-6700.

Instead of annual or daily fee passes, the park activities are individually fee-based. The activity fee can be purchased online, onsite or by telephone.

The park nature & interpretive centers are:

Eastman Nature Center, Dayton, 55369 (763-694-7700)
Richardson Nature Center, Bloomington, 55438
    (763-694-7676)
Carl W. Kroening Interpretive Center, Brooklyn Ctr., 55430.
    (763-694-7693)

Visit Three Rivers Park website and select Recreation Activities & Programs for each center's detailed webpage.

The Play Area at Hyland Lake Park Reserve is fondly known by visitors as chutes and ladders. Children and parents know it as lots of fun because of all the slides and ladders there. The longest slide is 50 feet and the shortest is 3 feet in the toddler playground. A newly added attraction, The Misters, are especially cooling for a run through on hot summer days. The play area is open dawn until dust. The park location is 10145 E. Bush Lake Rd., Bloomington. Within the park, the play area is south and west of the park's downhill ski area.

Elm Creek Park Reserve in Dayton has a swimming pond for summer enjoyment and tubing hill, snowboarding, down hill and cross country skiing for winter enjoyment. Swimming and tubing fees are $10 with skiing $4 to $20. Contact the park reserve's Visitor Center at 763-694-7894 for details.

*THUNDER SOCCER TEAM
James Griffin Stadium
275 N. Lexington Pkwy.
St. Paul, 55104

651-917-8326
www.mnthunder.com

Our Thunder professional soccer club season extends from May through September. The Twin Cities is fortunate to have such a very successful team that also goes out of its way to encourage and promote local youth soccer.

Special events are held throughout the season. And fans of all ages are invited onto the field after home games to meet and greet the players. Ticket prices are $8 for youth ages five through 17 and $12 for ages 18 and older.

In 2006, the **Minnesota Lightning**, a women's soccer team, was founded. Their home games are played at the Elizabeth Robbie Stadium on the University of Minnesota's St. Paul Campus at Cleveland Ave. and Larpenteur Ave. in Falcon Heights. Tickets are $6 for youth and $8 for adults.

Roll with the Thunder...It's a Ball!

Note: Kids Day, an annual event held on a Wednesday in late June always at 11 AM, is special. Besides special game ticket prices of $7 youth and $10 adult, there are children's games and prizes.

*TOUCH & SEE ROOM
Bell Museum of Natural History
University of Minnesota, Minneapolis Campus
10 Church St.
University Ave. & 17th Ave. S. E.
Minneapolis, 55455

612-624-7083 (infoline)
www.bellmuseum.org/touchandsee.html

In this special room everything is at child height and almost everything can be handled. There are skeletons, skins, bones and other animal parts for children to touch and examine. There are live snakes that can be handled with friendly staff supervision. There are even mounted antlers for children to try on for size. A corner of the room is set aside with large beanbag pillows and natural history books for children to read. The room is open Tuesday through Friday from 9 AM to 5 PM, Saturday from 10 AM to 5 PM and Sundays from noon to 5 PM. Admission to the Bell Museum is $5 for adults and $3 for children ages three to 16 and seniors except on Sundays when admission is free. No additional fees are charged for entering this special room.

TPT, INC.
172 E. 4th St.
St. Paul, 55101

651-222-1717
www.tpt.org

From November through April, tours for families with children ages five and up can be arranged at TPT (Twin Cities Public Television). The 30 minute tours take children into the studio and control rooms to see and hear about all the technical operations necessary to run the station.

Tours are given the first Saturday of the month from 10 AM until noon. Reservations are not needed.

*TRAIN RIDES AT OSCEOLA

Osceola & St. Croix Valley Railway
Minnesota Transportation Museum (MTM)
193 Pennsylvania Ave. E.
St. Paul, 55101

651-228-0263
715-755-3570 (Osceola)
www.trainride.org

Beginning in mid-April and continuing through October and only a short one hour drive from the Twin Cities, we can once again go for a short train ride in Osceola, WI. On weekends and holidays, the diesel passenger trains travel on routes to Marine on St. Croix, MN and Dresser, WI. All trains depart from the historic former Soo Line Depot on Depot Road and Hwy. 35 in Osceola, WI. The rides are 90 minutes round trip for a family fare of $40 for Marine on St. Croix trip and 50 minutes round trip for a family fare of $25 for the Dresser trip. Call or visit the website for schedules and other fare options, directions, reservation details and information on special events.

*TRAINS AT BANDANA SQUARE

Twin City Model Railroad Museum
Bandana Square
1021 Bandana Blvd. E.
St. Paul, 55108

651-647-9628
www.tcmrm.org

Climb the stairs to the second floor location for a wonderful exhibit of trains, trolleys and buildings presenting railroading in the United States during the 1930s, 1940s and 1950s. It includes reproductions of Twin Cities scenes such as the Como Shops and the St. Anthony Falls Milling District. In 3,500 square feet of space two double track main lines, one for passenger trains and one for freight, form the layout for the O scale model trains (one-quarter inch to the foot). Visiting hours are Tuesday through Thursday 11 AM to 3 PM, Friday 11 AM to 7 PM, Saturday from 10 AM to 6 PM and Sunday from noon to 5 PM. The museum's members, all volunteers, can be seen working on the exhibit Tuesday and Thursday evenings from 7 to 8:30. Especially nice for children is a railing with platforms which surrounds the layout. Children can stand on the platforms to see even better the trains and trolleys go by on the tracks. Admission is $3 for ages six and older. Five and under are admitted at no charge.

*TWINS BASEBALL
Humphrey Metrodome
34 Kirby Pucket Pl.
Minneapolis, 55415

612-33-TWINS (infoline)
800-33-TWINS
www.twinsbaseball.com

The Minnesota Twins, World Series Champions of 1987 and 1991, play ball from April to October in downtown Minneapolis. Knothole Days, Bat, Cap and other special days are held throughout the season to encourage families to attend a ball game.

Tickets range from $7 to $50. However, each season the Twins also offer a special adult and child promotional package that usually includes hot dogs and soft drinks with reduced ticket prices for most Thursday through Sunday games.

In late January, **TwinsFest** is held Friday through Sunday at the Metrodome. A family event, the Twins organization offers tours of the clubhouse, opportunities to meet current and past players and coaches, participate in fun baseball skills activities, etc.

Tickets range from $5 to $10 with a discount when purchased in advance. The event benefits the Minnesota Twins Community Fund that supports youth baseball and softball programs and is always well attended.

So let's all go to a ball game where fun is part of the game!

Note: During the baseball season, the Twins organization holds several free baseball clinics for boys and girls. These sessions focus on skills of defense, hitting, pitching and base running. Contact 612-33-TWINS for location and more information.

And try the website **www.playballminnesota.com** to locate baseball, softball and T-ball contacts for youth events and camps close to home in your area.

*UNDERWATER ADVENTURES AQUARIUM
Under the Mall of America East Entrance Level One
Interstate 494 & Hwy. 77
Bloomington, 55425

952-883-0202 (infoline)
www.sharky.tv

Awarded the World's Best Shark Encounter by the Discovery Channel, the aquarium is a showcase for over 4500 aquatic creatures including Brutus, a very large snapping turtle. Upon entering, look for the Daily Events & Feedings schedule for their times and locations. Could be "What's for lunch?" is one. The curved glass underwater tunnel contains fish of all sizes swimming above and on both sides as you move through it. Most interesting is to look up as a large fish swims above.

Pass through the gift shop and snack area to find the touch pool where children can actually touch shark and stingray and maybe find the horseshoe crab. A staff member explains the stingray is friendly. Its stinger is clipped. Look nearby for the tanks of baby stingrays and baby sharks..

Hours are Monday to Thursday from 10 AM to 8 PM, Friday and Saturday from 9:30 AM to 8:30 PM and Sunday from 10 AM to 7 PM. Admission prices are from $9.95 to $14.95. Children under three are free. Group rates are available for 20 people and up. Contact 952-853-0603 one week in advance of planned visit.

*UNIVERSITY OF MINNESOTA
Youth & Community Programs
104 St. Paul Campus Gymnasium
1536 N. Cleveland Ave.
St. Paul, 55108

612-625-2242 (infoline)
www.recsports.umn.edu/youth

The U's Department of Recreational Sports now offers several children's programs throughout the year. They include summer day camps, winter break sessions, learn to swim and birthday parties. Call and request the brochures that describe all the details including costs, age limitations, dates and locations. Information about the programs can also be found on the website.

UPPER ST. ANTHONY'S FALLS LOCK & DAM
Army Corps of Engineers
1 Portland Ave.
Minneapolis, 55401

1-877-552-1416
www.mvp.usace.army.mil

Now only prebooked tours are available. Scheduled from 10 AM to 6 PM during the navigation season usually beginning in May and continuing into October most years, children, who must be accompanied by an adult, will find viewing the locks below most interesting. And with luck may see a boat come through.

To schedule a tour e-mail **dam.tours@usace.army.mil** or call. Information requested includes contact and how to reach, size and age of tour and date and time desired.

Note: Lock & Dam No. 1, a newly discovered yet long-time existing lock & dam, also known as the Ford Dam, does have a public access observation deck. Open the end of May through October, its at 5000 W. River Road, south of Ford Bridge. Look for signage. Parking is limited. Call 612-724-2971 in April for updates.

*VALLEYFAIR FAMILY AMUSEMENT PARK
One Valleyfair Drive
State Hwy. 101
Shakopee, 55379

952-445-7600 or 952-445-6500 (infoline)
1-800-386-7433
www.valleyfair.com

"For the Biggest Family Day Around" visit the delightful family amusement park, Valleyfair. Located on 90 acres of land three miles east of Shakopee, it is open seven days a week from mid-May through Labor Day and then weekends in September and October. Both children and adults will find this an enjoyable and sparkling clean entertaining place to visit. Plan at least six hours to see and do it all. Don't miss driving the antique autos and riding on the authentic 1925 carousel which was originally built for the Excelsior Minnesota Amusement Park.

There are many activity areas planned especially for children of 54 inches or shorter. They include the Rub-a-Dub Tubs water ride for the very young and the Half-Pint Park with a seaplane ride, train ride and hot air balloon ride. Another area features a miniature carousel. Kid-Works has the foamball factory, fun for all family members and the rockin-tug attraction. Other favorites are the bumper cars and the family roller coaster ride, Mad Mouse. For the adventurous family, the Log Flume is particularly nice on a hot day as you ride down water-filled chutes and get wet. The Corkscrew is a head-over-heels experience for the brave.

Note: For safety precautions, all rides have height requirements that are posted at each ride's entrance.

The **Pepsi IMAX Theater** located on the grounds inside Valleyfair features a spectacular film on its huge screen. To find out what the current season's show is and for show times, check their website or pickup a brochure on the park grounds.

Finally, step aboard the Minnesota River Valley Railroad for a train ride around the park grounds.

General admission to the park is $33.95. Children three years and older and less than 48 inches tall are admitted for $9.95. Seniors are $9.95 also. Children two and under are free. Admission includes access to rides and shows. Some attractions and Challenge Park have additional admission fees. Parking is $8. Valleyfair hours are 10 AM to varying closing times of 6 to 12 PM depending on the day of the week and season of the year. Call or check the website.

Whitewater Country Waterpark located on the Valleyfair grounds is a special attraction with no additional admission fee charged for entrance and enjoyment. Tubes are available to ride down long, wet chutes of water. Bring your own bathing suits and towels. Lockers are available for a partial refundable fee. This is loads of fun judging by the many smiling faces seen the day we visited.

VISION OF PEACE
St. Paul City Hall/Ramsey County Court House
Memorial Hall
15 W. Kellogg Blvd.
St. Paul, 55102

Carl Milles, the well-known sculptor, created this work of art from the concept of Native Americans gathering in council to smoke their sacred pipes. Rising from the smoke of the pipe, Milles envisioned a "god of peace" statue which he sculpted holding a sacred pipe and extending a hand in friendship.

Children seem in awe of this huge, 36-foot tall statue when they first view it. Sculpted from white Mexican onyx and weighing 55 tons, it rotates very slowly 132 degrees. The building is open from 8 AM to 4:30 PM

Monday through Friday. Group tours can be arranged by calling 651-266-8002. There are no group size or age limitations.

Note: An excellent, informative self-guided tour flyer is also available on site in the Citizens Service Office, room 110. It contains lots of interesting details about the newly renovated Concourse Level, i.e. basement. And do as it suggests. Ask the guard to start the glass mural's light show.

NOTES

*WALKER ART CENTER
1750 Hennepin Ave.
Minneapolis, 55403

612-375-7600 (infoline)
http://learn.walkerart.org

Many programs for children are offered throughout the year at the new Walker Art Center. New because a wing was added to the building in 2005. It includes two interactive education tools, a holographic dolphin with artificial intelligence and an arcade-like audio video fractoid machine. To interact with these alone are worth a visit.

Summer's Cool, a summer arts program, in June, July and August offers classes for children ages three and older. The offerings are on weekdays and Thursday evenings which is nice for working parents. The individual class and tuition fees range from $30 to $240. Call the summer's school hotline at 612-253-3432 beginning in early March to request a Summer's Cool brochure. The department hours are Monday through Friday from 10 AM to 5 PM. The website also has the details beginning in March.

Family, school and other groups can schedule a tour of the Walker by calling 612-375-7609. Three weeks advance notice is needed.

The art center hours are Tuesday through Sundays from 11 AM to 5 PM except on Thursday and Friday when open until 9 PM. It is closed on Monday. Admission is $8 for adults, $6 for seniors and $4 for students. Children 12 and under are free. Admission to the Walker is free for everyone Thursday evenings from 5 PM to 9 PM.

Note: Free First Saturdays are for families. This is a full day of family art fun. Held on the first Saturday of the month from 10 AM to 5 PM, family activities are planned with a new theme for each event. There is always a hands-on art activity. Other happenings could include a film, art tour, dance performance and storytelling. Members receive the Walker, a bi-monthly publication listing the upcoming themes and dates. Information can also be found at Calendar on website.

*WARNER NATURE CENTER
15375 Norell Ave. N.
Marine-on-St. Croix, 55047

651-433-2427
www.smm.org/warnernaturecenter

The center, located in the St. Croix Valley, operates in association with the Science Museum of Minnesota. Most of the programs are planned for children in elementary grades and up. However, public events include family programs for children as young as two. Seasonal education and recreation classes are offered all year around. There's snowshoe adventure, fall canoe, spring maple syruping and family camping to list a few. For current and upcoming descriptions of the many wonderful programs, contact the center for a brochure. The website has information, too. All programs require pre-registration. Fees range from $5 to $155.

Note: Mothers and dads, scout leaders, educators and others are encourages to arrange visits as part of a school science program or badge requirement or church school experience. Also birthday party packages and summer camp programs are available.

*WAY-COOL COOKING SCHOOL
16544 W. 78th St.
Eden Prairie, 55344

952-949-6799
www.waycoolcookingschool.com

The school offers lots of choices for children from ages four and up. With emphasis on fun and healthy eating, the complete listing of cooking classes and events (including some for adults) is on their website. Fees for classes begin at $25 and up per child. Birthday party packages start at $230.

At a recent class making spaghetti sauce, the children learned that by crushing the Italian seasonings before adding releases their oils resulting in a sauce that's "better than in the can" according to one small chef's taste test. The class went on to make cheesy garlic bread and smoothies in a bag. And then they enjoyed it all for lunch.

With humor added to the informative teaching and with many helpers, groups of even 40 can be accommodated at this lively, yet well organized school.

WCCO TELEVISION STUDIOS
Communications Dept.
90 S. 11th St.
Minneapolis, 55403

612-339-4444
www.wcco.com

Children ten and older can tour the station. Stops include air control , the control room, newsroom, weather center and studio. Tours are scheduled Monday through Friday at 10 AM and 2 PM. The tours last about 30 to 45 minutes. Groups of five to 15 can be accommodated.

Note: The new newsroom set now is visible through glass windows from the sidewalks of Nicollet Mall. Stop by and look in.

WESTWOOD HILLS NATURE CENTER
8300 W. Franklin Ave.
St. Louis Park, 55426

952-924-2544
www.stlouispark.org

Over three miles of paved and woodchip trails wind through a marsh at this 150 acre environmental center. There is a quarter mile floating board-walk crossing a lake for walkers, hikers and explorers to enjoy. The center is owned and operated by the City of St. Louis Park. The Interpretative Center building is open from 8 AM to 4:30 PM weekdays year around and on weekends from noon to 5 PM September through May.

Exhibits change with the season. There is maple syruping in the spring and pond life in summer and others which change from time to time. Something new is happening here everyday.

A naturalist led tour can be scheduled for school and youth groups as well as family groups. Special events are held on a regular basis throughout the year. A few of the programs have a small fee. To be put on a mailing to receive the center's seasonal listing of programs, contact them. And the bird watching continues to be excellent at the Westwood Hills Nature Center according to the center's naturalist.

The center has a Wild Flower Trail that is a quarter mile accessible paved trail leading through wild flower fields and past a frog pond..croak,croak. Look for the honeybee apiary along the way. Trial hours are dawn to dusk year around.

Note: Birthday parties can be scheduled on Saturdays and Sundays with advance reservations a must. For party time, the center provides a room, a brief introduction to the area and a naturalist-led hike and other activities. The resident fee is $65 and non-resident $75 for reserved parties. The birthday treats are supplied by the party givers.

WHOLE KIDS CLUB
Whole Foods Market
30 S. Fairview Ave.
St. Paul, 55105

651-690-0197
www.wholefoodsmarket.com/stores

There are lots of healthy and free perks for children of age three to 12 for becoming a member of this unique new club including a fresh fruit tart coupon just for joining. On Thursdays, show the membership card and receive a treat. VIP special events by invitation are held throughout the year. Attend the events to collect the wooden tokens for redeeming for prizes like a balsam wooden airplane to a Kids Club apron with chef hat.

The store also provides tours upon request. The child friendly tour guide will introduce the many food choices and fresh produce products to children in the half hour tour. Beginning in the bakery with a small cookie snack, the tour continues to the produce section where one meets Craig, the stuffed monkey. He talks about bananas, of course. In the deli section, children can select an item to sample. A slice of fresh pizza was the favorite on our tour. The large international food aisle is fascinating with many Japanese and Asian items to learn about. The tour concludes with another treat such as a frozen fruit bar offered to all and receipt of the collectable wooden token.

All events and visits require the children be accompanied by an adult.

WILD RUMPUS
Books for Young Readers
2720 W. 43rd St.
Minneapolis, 55410

612-920-5005
www.wildrumpusbooks.com

This children's bookstore has special Saturday events that begin at 1 PM and end when "you say WHEN!" Past events have included a sheepshearer, a forensic entomologist and a rodeo star. Some events need reservations. Contact Wild Rumpus for event information or visit the website and look for Upcoming Wild Times. And what's unique? Shelves of recycled books for $.25 to $1 a book. And what's weird? Look for the floor grate to see the rats living beneath the floorboards.

WOOD LAKE NATURE CENTER
Richfield Park & Recreation Dept.
6710 Lake Shore Dr.
Richfield, 55423

612-861-9365
www.ci.richfield.mn.us

Wood Lake Nature Center is an exciting place for children and adults to explore together. Seasonal and topical tours for families and individuals are given on a scheduled basis Saturday and Sunday and some weekday evenings. Special seasonal activities and classes ranging from astronomy to whole earth cookery and including snowshoe making and honey extraction are offered throughout the year. All have space limitations requiring reservations in advance. Some have small fees. For more detailed information, contact the center and request the seasonal flyer that lists all their classes and events or visit the website. Also available at the center are self-guiding materials that include a trail map and bird list.

Except for holidays, the center is open all year. The building hours are from Monday through Saturday 8:30 AM to 5 PM and Sunday noon to 5 PM. The grounds hours are from sunrise to 11 PM.

XCEL ENERGY
Public Safety Demonstrations
Corporate Headquarters
414 Nicollet Mall
Minneapolis, 55401

612-330-1962
www.xcelenergy.com

The safety demonstrations given by retired Xcel/NSP employees are very powerful. The presenter brings a demonstration kit from which he or she then sets up situations showing how to safely act around power lines. They show what to do if in a car near a downed power line and talk about kite flying near power lines. The program, which lasts from 45 minutes to an hour, is for school, scout and other groups of children of third grade age and older. Call between 8 AM and 4 PM weekdays and ask for the public safety dept. to arrange for this unique visit. It is best to schedule at least two weeks in advance.

Note: The Xcel Bird Cam on their website is a link to the peregrine falcon Raptor Resource Project. In the spring, this is a fun and educational way to monitor the activity of a growing peregrine falcon family.

*YMCA OF GREATER ST. PAUL & YMCA OF METROPOLITAN MINNEAPOLIS
www.ymcatwincities.org

Family, preschool and youth classes and programs are offered at most of the Y locations listed. Swimming, gymnastics, day camps, ballet, karate and skateboarding are just some of the many to choose from. Contact any of the Y's to receive a current catalog of information on classes, dates, fee and special events. The website is useful, too. Select Current Program Guide for the Y of interest.

Kids Stuff is a drop-in center for children ages six weeks to ten. Activities are planned that may include games, storytelling, arts and crafts and free play. The Y describes it as "a special place that kids can call their own" while Mom and Dad get some exercise time too. Member's children are free for up to two hours. The fee for a guest child is $4 per hour. The Kids Stuff Parent Handbook contains the guidelines for use of the center.

The **Voyager** programs are designed especially for parents and children in kindergarten through seventh grade to have active fun together. The programs are organized within neighborhoods by child's age group and offered during the school year. Program fees begin at $25.

Super Family Sundays! is a new program that rotates among Y branch locations. The hosting Y plans an afternoon of family fun with snacks and activities for all.

We build strong kids, strong families, strong communities.

St. Paul area locations:
East: 875 Arcade, 55106 (651-771-8881)
Midway: 1761 University Ave., 55104 (651-646-4557)
Northeast in White Bear Lake: 2100 Orchard Lane, 55110
   (651-777-8103)
Northwest: 3760 N. Lexington, 55126 (651-483-2671)
South in W. St. Paul: 150 E. Thompson Ave., 55118 (651-457-0048)
Southeast in Woodbury: 2175 Radio Dr., 55125 (651-731-9507)
Southwest in Eagan: 550 Opperman Dr., 55123 (651-456-9622)
Minneapolis area locations:
Blaisdell: 3335 Blaisdell Ave. S., 55408 (612-827-5401)
Emma B. Howe-Northtown in Coon Rapids:
   8950 Springbrook Dr., 55433 (763-785-7882)
Minnesota Valley in Burnsville: 13850 Portland Ave. S., 55337
   (952-898-9622)
Northwest in New Hope: 7601 42nd Ave. N., 55427 (763-535-4800)
Ridgedale in Minnetonka: 12301 Ridgedale Dr., 55305 (952-544-7708)
Southdale in Edina: 7355 York Ave. S., 55435 (952-835-2567)

Join one—join them all—with an adult one month membership for $55.

111

*YOUTH PERFORMANCE COMPANY (YPC)
610 W. 28th St.
Minneapolis, 55408

612-623-9080 (infoline)
www.youthperformanceco.com

YPC presents four to five new stories each season. These are often familiar tales but done in original, often humorous ways. Seusical and Paul Bunyan & Other Minne-Tales have been performed in original adaptations. Serious plays have included MVP-The Jackie Robinson Story based on the life of this American hero. Most plays are recommended for children of age seven or eight and older with at least one of the series for all ages.

Performances are at the Howard Conn Fine Arts Center, 1900 Nicollet Ave. S. in Minneapolis, 55403. Ticket prices begin at $10 for adults and $8 for seniors and children 14 and under. Ticket discounts are available for groups of 20 or more. Show days vary but times are usually 10 AM and 12:30 PM weekdays and 2 PM and 7:30 PM on weekends. Visit the website or call for a seasonal performance brochure.

Saturday and summer classes on theatre arts are offered. Contact YPC for the current classes and costs. For the summer production, children not only do the performing but they help write the script and music. They can get involved in making the costumes and sets, too.

*THE ZOO
13000 Zoo Blvd.
Apple Valley, 55124

952-431-9200 or 952-431-9500 (infoline)
1-800-366-7811
www.mnzoo.org

Open all year, the Minnesota Zoo visitors can discover and enjoy over 2100 animals and see thousands of plants in exhibits representing the natural habitats of the animals and birds. Several trips a year are needed to see and participate in all the activities of the zoo. Upon entering the main building, check the Guest Services Desk for a listing of the daily events. This could include times for animal feedings, special shows, tours and other announcements for the day. Then plan at least four hours of delightful discoveries. But don't miss out on seeing the dolphins, our favorites. The tropical room is especially pleasant on a cold winter day for its lush, colorful vegetation.

Open during the warm weather months, the Wells Fargo Family Farm is where children can see and touch and experience life in a farm setting. On the grounds are a farmhouse, chicken house, swine barn, machine shed, goat and sheep barn and a grain elevator. In the elevator, children can pretend to be grain as they climb and slide into the bins.

A special attraction is the World of Birds with its several daily shows. On the Northern Trial area of the zoo is where the tigers, musk oxen, camels, wild horses and moose live outdoors all year around. Walking paths wind through this area. Or ride through it on the monorail for $3.50.

The zoo opens at 9 AM with closing time varying with the season of the year. Admission is $12 for adults, $8.25 for seniors, $7 for ages three through twelve and free for children two and under. Zoo members are admitted free. Parking is $5. Group rates are available for 20 or more with advance reservations by calling 952-431-9228 to reach the Group Sales office.

The zoo offers a number of programs to acquaint school age children with the animals. Either arrangements can be made for the school to come to the zoo for learning excursions, self-guided tours and special classes or the zoo will travel to the school with its Zoomobile. For all the details including fees, contact the Zoo Scheduler at 952-431-9228. Much of the information about the programs is also on their website.

NOTES

DAY TRIPS

DAY TRIPS

These activities are located outside the Twin Cities. Plan at least a day's adventure for exploring.

*CHARLES A. LINDBERGH HISTORIC SITE
1620 Lindbergh Dr. S.
Little Falls, 56345

1-320-616-5421
www.mnhs.org/places/sites/lh

Located in Charles A. Lindbergh State Park, which is two miles south of Little Falls, the Lindbergh house is the boyhood home of Minnesota's famous aviator. The house was built in 1906 by his father and is kept as it was in 1927. Visitors can tour the house and the visitor's center. Special events are held on selected weekends throughout the summer.

The hours are Tuesday through Saturday from 10 AM to 5 PM and noon to 5 PM on Sunday from May through Labor Day. From then through October, the hours are Saturdays from 10 AM to 4 PM and Sundays from noon to 4 PM. Admission is from $4 to $7.

*COMSTOCK HOUSE
506 8th St. S.
Moorhead, 56560

1-218-233-4211
www.mnhs.org/places/sites/ch

On Hwy. 75 in Moorhead, a half mile north of the Hwy. I-94 exit, the Comstock House can be found. It is noted for being the home of two important Minnesotans, Solomon G. Comstock, a politician and businessman in this upper Red River Valley area for over 60 years and his daughter, Ada Comstock, the first dean of women at the University of Minnesota and then president of Radcliffe College from 1923 to 1943.

The house was built in 1882/83 and has been restored to portray the living conditions of that time. Guided tours tell the history of the Red River Valley and about the lives of the Comstocks.

Hours are from 1 to 4:30 PM weekends and from 5 to * PM Tuesdays from the end of May through Labor Day. Other times can be arranged for groups through advance reservations. Admission is from $2 to $4.

*FOREST HISTORY CENTER
2609 Cty. Rd. 76
Grand Rapids, 55744

1-218-327-4482
www.mnhs.org/places/sites/fhc

Located near Hwys. 169 and 2 West, the center shows with living history characters how the lumberjack lived at the turn of the century. This site features a logging camp with a fire tower, a floating cook shack used for log drives and a forest ranger cabin. There are over two miles of self-guided forest trails and museum exhibits to explore as well. This is a wonderful place to visit to hear the story of how people lived in the forests of Minnesota from ancient times to the present. Special events are held on some weekends.

From June through Labor Day, the logging camp and center are open from 10 AM to 5 PM Monday through Saturday and noon to 5 PM on Sunday. After Labor Day through May, only the trails and museum exhibits are open weekdays. Call for hours. Other times can be arranged for groups through advance reservations. Admission is from $4 to $7.

*FORT RIDGELY
R.R.1, Box 65A
Fairfax, 55332

1-507-426-7888
www.mnhs.org/places/sites/fr

Located in Fort Ridgely State Park, which is seven miles south of Fairfax off Hwy. 4, Minnesota's third military post was closed and its buildings torn down after the U.S.-Dakota Indians Conflict of 1862. These building materials were then taken and used by the settlers to build their homes and barns. Today, a restored stone commissary is on the site. The visitor center has exhibits that help explain Fort Ridgely's history. Some remnants of the original buildings also remain for exploring. Special events are held on several summer weekends.

The site is open Memorial Day through Labor Day Friday and Saturday from 10 AM to 5 PM and Sunday from noon to 5 PM. And then with the same hours on weekends only through October. Daily admission is $2 for adults. Also a state park vehicle permit is required.

*GREAT LAKES AQUARIUM (GLA)
353 Harbor Dr.
Duluth, 55802

1-218-740-3474
1-877-866-3474
www.glaquarium.org

The Great Lakes Aquarium is more than an exhibit of fish in tanks. There are many exhibits of historical events that have taken place on or near Lake Superior, too. The aquarium, the only freshwater aquarium in the United States, opened the summer of 2000 and is still evolving. There are at least 70 species of freshwater fish as well as birds and ducks.

The Wall of Water at the lobby entrance is impressive. Pick up a copy of the Secrets of the Water Wall flier that explains the many graphic symbols on the wall.

Also pick up the aquarium's daily schedule for the times and locations when special programs like Stingray Snacktime are held. On a recent visit a snake skin (without the snake) and turtle shell (without the turtle) were passed around for close-up looks during the Remarkable Reptiles program. With proper instructions for touching the live python snake given, all were invited to line-up to do so.

Children's favorites will include Zhoosh, the otter, in Otter Cove. Zhoosh means slide in Ojibway. The Water Table set-up for piloting small boats through locks is another favorite. At the Touch and See tank, a freshwater stingray can be stroked and a baby sturgeon petted. And piloting a virtual ore boat under the Aerial Lift Bridge was a serious experience for a six year old as she then continued to carefully steer between the piers and onto the Lake.

Hours are from 10 AM to 6 PM every day of the year. Admission is $12.95 for adults, $9.95 for seniors, $6.95 for children ages three to eleven and free for children under three. Parking is $3. To reach the aquarium, take Exit 256B from Hwy. I-35 to the large blue, green and red building near the waterfront.

Note: Special events are held throughout the year. At the Fish Fest, children could make a fish hat and snack on fish gummies and crackers. Birthday party packages with special rates for groups of ten or more are available, too.

*JEFFERS PETROGLYPHS HISTORIC SITE
27160 Cty. Rd. 2
Comfrey, 56019

1-507-628-5591
www.mnhs.org/places/sites/jp

Located three miles east of Hwy. 71 on Cottonwood Cty. Rd. 10, then one mile south on Cty. Rd. 2, this is the site of over 2000 carvings of human figures, weapons and animals made by North American Indians on ancient quartzite rocks. It is thought that some of the carvings date back to 3000 BC while others are as new as the 18th century. A visitor's center on the grounds contains an exhibit that helps to explain some of the carvings. It also describes the surrounding prairie ecology.

The hours for visiting are from 10 AM to 5 PM Monday through Friday, on Saturday 10 AM to 8 PM and noon to 5 PM Sunday from Memorial Day through Labor Day. May and September hours are to 5 PM weekends only. Other months open by reservations. Admission is from $3 to $5.

*LAKE SUPERIOR & MISSISSIPPI RAILROAD (LSMR)
PO Box 16211
Duluth, 55816

1-218-624-7549
www.lsmrr.org

This train ride is a recent discovery. However, for many years now it has been providing scenic rides along the St. Louis River on track built in 1870 to connect Duluth with the Twin Cities. On the 12 mile round trip, passengers may see bears, beavers, deer and many different birds like ducks, geese and herons. The ride can be described as a "nature walk on rails."

Operated since 1981 by a group of dedicated volunteers from the Lake Superior Transportation Club, the members are continually working on maintaining the vintage coach cars, a bright yellow locomotive and the open air flat green Safari car.

Tickets are purchased at the white and blue Excursion Train booth where one can also purchase train souvenirs like T-shirts, whistles, engineer hats and spikes. Tickets are $9 for adults and $6 for children ages four to eleven. Departures are at 10:30 AM and 1:30 PM weekends from mid-June to early October. The ride is an hour and half long.

To locate the railroad coming from the Twin Cities on Hwy. I-35 exit at 251A and make right turns on 63rd Ave. W and then Grand Ave. Look for their sign across from the Zoo. From Duluth on Hwy. I-35 exit left to Grand Ave. (251B) and go west to sign. Parking is available in their large adjacent lot.

Note: The train can be chartered for birthday parties. And a fall color tour is very popular.

*LAKE SUPERIOR ZOO
7210 Fremont St.
72nd Ave. W. & Grand Ave.
Duluth, 55807

1-218-730-4900
www.lszoo.org

Upon entering the zoo, pickup the colorful Explore Zoo brochure with handy map of attractions. Also located in the entrance is the daily feeding schedules. Then plan to spend the next one and one-half to two hours exploring this easy to walk around and friendly staffed attraction.

In the Grigg's Learning Center, visitors are asked questions at displays like "What is a Reptile?" with answers provided. Here also are insects and small animals in glass houses. Look closely for the giant stick insect as large it is not.

In the Nocturnal exhibit we watched the bats being fed cut fruits and fruit juices. And were told that if a bat is flying around us in the out of doors it is after the hovering mosquitoes. Go bats!

Trouble, a Kodiak bear, became our favorite. He came to the Duluth zoo from an Alaskan zoo where he was a trouble maker having eaten too many flamingos.

Open every day year around (except certain holidays) the summer hours are 10 AM to 5 PM and winter hours are 10 AM to 4 PM. Admission is $8 for ages 13 and older and $3 for children ages three to twelve.

The zoo is ten minutes from Duluth at the base of West Duluth's Spirit Mountain in Fairmont Park. Going north towards Duluth on Hwy. I-35 exit on Cody St. (251A) and follow the signs.

Note: Educational fun activities like Scout Programs, Zoo Snooze: An Overnight Adventure and seasonal Adventure Classes are offered, too. For details on these, call the education office at 218-723-3854.

*LOWER SIOUX AGENCY
32469 Redwood Cty. Hwy. 2
Morton, 56270

1-507-697-6321
www.mnhs.org/places/sites/lsa

Located on Hwy. 2 nine miles east of Redwood Falls is a stone warehouse that today marks the site of the agency. This historic location was where the first organized Indian attack in the U.S.-Dakota Conflict of 1862 took place. A visitor's center tells the story of the Dakota Indians struggle against the white settlers whose building of farms reduced their hunting grounds and fur trading activities.

The hours are 10 AM to 5 PM Friday and Saturday and noon to 5 PM Sunday from Memorial Day through Labor Day. Group tours at other times can be arranged. Special events are held some summer weekends. Admission is from $3 to $5.

*MILLE LACS INDIAN MUSEUM
Hwy. 169
Onamia, 56359

1-320-532-3632
www.mnhs.org

Located on Hwy. 169 on the southwest shore of Mille Lacs Lake 12 miles north of Onamia, this is the site of a museum and a restored trading post that have crafts and exhibits showing Ojibway culture.

Hours are 10 AM to 6 PM daily from Memorial Day through Labor Day. Off-season hours are 11 AM to 4 PM Friday through Monday in May and September. The trading post is open October through April Thursday through Saturday from 11 AM to 4 PM except when closed for the month of January. Admission is from $4 to $7.

*NORTH SHORE SCENIC RAILROAD
The Depot
506 W. Michigan St.
Duluth, 55802

1-218-722-1273 or 1-218-733-7590
1-800-423-1273
www.northshorescenicrailroad.org

As third generation members of a DM&IR railroad family, trains and train rides are very special to us; thus it is very nice to continue to be able to write about this activity. There are presently several different train ride choices. The Lester River ride is a one and one-half hour long round trip with two or three scheduled each day. The cost is $11 for adults and $5 for children ages three to 13.

The Two Harbors ride is a six hour round trip that includes a two hour layover in Two Harbors for exploring this pleasant town. This once a day scheduled trip begins at 10:30 AM Friday and Saturday. The cost is $20 for adults and $10 for children ages three through 13.

Pizza train rides are also regularly scheduled offerings. And special fall color trips are planned in September and October at the times the leaves are changing. Reservations are required for all but the Lester River rides.

Presently, the train rides are scheduled from mid-May through October. But because this is such a time-dependent adventure, confirming days and times is important to avoid disappointment.

Note: Birthday parties on the Birthday Caboose can be scheduled. The cost is $150 and includes the Lester River ride with pizza and cake. Call for the details.

*NORTH WEST COMPANY FUR POST
Box 51
Pine City, 55063

1-320-629-6356
www.mnhs.org/places/sites/nwcfp

Located on Hwy. 7 one and a half miles west of Hwy. I-35 at exit 169, the site has recreated the 1804 post that for one winter was home for the trappers of the British North West Company.

After a short walk from the parking area along the Snake River, one is greeted on the grounds of the post by men and women dressed in the clothing of this recreated era. The day we explored, we were invited by Angelique, our guide, to taste freshly prepared fry bread. It had been cooked over an open wood fire near the stockade fences entrance.

Costumed guides shares fascinating stories about life on the post. Much detail is given because of the journals which were kept by Mr. Sayers, the North West Company's representative at the post. At the reconstructed Wintering Post, a clerk explains the system of fur trade barter. It has many animal pelts hanging from the ceiling. These pelts are representative of the kinds traded and it was fun guessing the animals they came from. On the shelves were sponges, cloth, tools and beads. These were some of the items used to trade for the pelts.

The post is open Monday through Saturday from 10 AM to 5 PM and Sunday noon to 5 PM May through Labor Day. After Labor Day through October the post is open Friday through Sunday hours only. Other times can be arranged for groups through advance reservations. Admission is from $4 to $7.

*OLIVER H. KELLEY FARM
15788 Kelley Farm Rd.
Elk River, 55330

763-441-6896
www.mnhs.org/places/sites/ohkf

Located on Hwy. 10 West two and a half miles southeast of Elk River, this is the site of the founding of the Patrons of the Grange in 1867. It is now a living history farm that depicts farm life of the 1860s and 70s. Guides dressed in period clothing till the fields with oxen, horses and 19th century farm tools. The visitors center features an exhibit about Mr. Kelley and the Grange. Special events are held most weekends.

The farm and visitor center are open Tuesday through Saturday from 10 AM to 5 PM and Sunday from noon to 5 PM from late May through Labor Day. In May, September and October, it is open on weekend hours only. Admission is from $4 to $7.

*SPLIT ROCK LIGHTHOUSE HISTORIC SITE
3713 Split Rock Lighthouse Rd.
Two Harbors, 55616

1-218-226-6372
www.mnhs.org/splitrock

Located in Split Rock Lighthouse State Park on Hwy. 61, 20 miles northeast of Two Harbors, the site includes the brick light tower, a fog-signal building, several lighthouse keepers' homes and the ruins of a tramway. The story of the lighthouse and development of the North Shore is shown on a video and in an exhibit at the visitors center. The lighthouse was built in 1910 and was in use for nearly 60 years. Special events are held on several weekends during the year.

Hours are 10 AM to 6 PM daily from mid-May through mid-October. Admission is from $4 to $8. From January to mid-May on weekends only, the visitor center is open 11 AM to 4 PM. Other times can be arranged for groups with advance reservations. There is no admission fee then but a state park vehicle permit is required.

*S. S. WILLIAM A. IRVIN ORE BOAT MUSEUM
350 Harbor Dr.
Duluth Downtown Waterfront at Lake Ave.
Duluth, 55802

1-218-722-7876
www.williamairvin.com

Tours of the Irvin are offered from May through October. For more than 40 years, the ship carried iron ore and coal on the Great Lakes and was once the flagship of the U.S. Steel's Great Lakes Fleet. It was retired because it was too small. However, a tour with very informative guides, makes that hard to believe. We thought it huge, especially the cargo holds.

The Irvin is longer than two football fields and the cargo area has enough space for 200 rail cars. For this tour, wear good walking shoes.

The 60 minute tour costs $9 for adults and $6 for children ages twelve and under. A tour of Sundew, a U.S. Coast Guard Cutter, is included with the fee. Parking is $3 at the Duluth Entertainment Convention Center (DECC) which is next to the Irvin.

Helpful websites, telephone numbers and addresses for planning visits to explore attractions outside the Twin Cities are listed here. And current road conditions and weather report information is available from the Minnesota Department of Transportation by calling 1-800-542-0220 or by visiting their website **www.511mn.org**

EXPLORE MINNESOTA TOURISM
100 Metro Sq., 121 7th Pl. E., St. Paul, 55101
651-296-5029 or 1-800-657-3700
www.exploreminnesota.com
Friendly contacts for planning regional travel including information on parks, campgrounds, boat rentals, resorts and festivals.

AUSTIN CONVENTION & VISITORS BUREAU/CVB
104 11th Ave. N.W., Austin, 55912
1-800-444-5713
www.austincvb.com
Attractions: Spam Museum, SpamFest

BRAINERD LAKES AREA CHAMBER OF COMMERCE/CVB
PO Box 356, 124 N. 6th St., Brainerd, 56401
1-800-450-2838
www.brainerd.com
Attractions: Paul Bunyan Nature Learning Center, Paul Bunyan Trail, Paul Bunyan Land at This Old Farm Pioneer Village

CHISHOLM AREA CHAMBER OF COMMERCE
223 W. Lake St., Chisholm, 55719
1-800-422-0806
www.chisholmchamber.com
Attractions: Iron World Discovery Center, Minnesota Museum of Mining

VISIT DULUTH
21 W. Superior St. Suite 100, Duluth, 55802
1-800-438-5884
www.visitduluth.com
Attractions: The Depot, Lake Superior Zoo, Lakewalk, Park Point, Playfront, Spirit Mountain

ELY CHAMBER OF COMMERCE
1600 E. Sheridan St., Ely, 55731
1-800-777-7281
www.ely.org
Attractions: BWCA, International Wolf Center

FARGO/MOORHEAD CONVENTION & VISITORS BUREAU/CVB
PO BOX 2164, 2001 44th St. S.W., Fargo, ND 58103
1-800-235-7654
www.fargomoorhead.org
Attractions: Comstock House, Heritage Hjemkonst Interpretive Center

GRAND MARAIS AREA TOURISM
PO Box 1048, 13 N. Broadway, Grand Marais, 55604
1-888-922-5000
www.grandmaraismn.com
Attractions: Gunflint Trail

GRAND RAPIDS TOURISM
501 S. Pokegama Ave., Grand Rapids, 55744
1-800-355-9740
www.visitgrandrapids.com
Attractions: Forest History Center, Judy Garland Museum & Birthplace

INTERNATIONAL FALLS CONVENTION & VISITORS BUREAU/CVB
301 2nd Ave., International Falls, 56649
1-800-325-5766
www.rainylake.org
Attractions: Gold Mine, Ice Box Days, Smokey Bear

LAKE CITY AREA CHAMBER OF COMMERCE
101 W. Center St., Lake City, 55041
1-800-369-4123
www.lakecity.org
Attractions: Frontenac State Park, Hok-Si-La

LITTLE FALLS CONVENTION & VISITORS BUREAU/CVB
606 S.E. 1st St., Little Falls, 56345
1-800-325-5916
www.littlefallsmn.com
Attractions: Camp Ripley, Charles A. Lindbergh Visitor Center, Charles
Weyerhaeuser Museum, Fishing Museum

GREATER MANKATO AREA CHAMBER OF COMMERCE/CVB
PO Box 999, 112 Riverfront Dr., Mankato, 56002
1-800-657-4733
www.greatermankato.com
Attractions: Betsy-Tacy Self-Guided Walking Tours

MILLE LACS AREA TOURISM
PO Box 758, 204 Roosevelt Rd. S., Onamia, 56359
1-888-350-2692
www.millelacs.com
Attractions: Father Hennepin State Park, Mille Lacs Indian Museum

NEW ULM CHAMBER OF COMMERCE/CVB
PO Box 384, 1 N. Minnesota, New Ulm, 56073
1-888-463-9856
www.newulm.com
Attractions: Bavarian Blast, Town Square Glokenspiel

PIPESTONE CHAMBER & VISITORS BUREAU
PO Box 8, 117 8th Ave. S.E., Pipestone, 56164
1-800-336-6125
www.pipestoneminnesota.com
Attractions: Fort Pipestone, Peace Pipe at Rock Island Depot, Pipestone National Monument, Song of Hiawatha Pageant, Pipestone County Museum, National Monument

REDWOOD FALLS AREA CHAMBER & TOURISM
PO Box 21, 200 S. Mill St., Redwood Falls, 56283
1-800-657-7070
www.redwoodfalls.org
Attractions: Fort Ridgely History Center, Laura Ingalls Wilder Museum, Lower Sioux Agency History Site, Sod House on the Prairie

TWO HARBORS AREA CHAMBER OF COMMERCE
1313 Fairgrounds Rd., Two Harbors, 55616
1-800-777-7384
www.twoharborschamber.com
Attractions: Ore Docks, Split Rock Lighthouse, Two by Two Historic Self-Guided Walking Tour

WINDOM AREA CHAMBER OF COMMERCE/CVB
303 9th St., Windom, 56101
1-800-794-6366
www.winwacc.com
Attractions: Jeffers Petroglyphs

NOTES

SEASONAL EVENTS

SEASONAL EVENTS

For up-to-date information on the event, check the local newspapers, websites and/or call during the season.

SPRING

CINCO DE MAYO FIESTA - May
Riverview Economic Development Association (REDA)
176 Cesar Chavez
St. Paul, 55107

651-222-6347
www.districtdelsol.com

Cinco de Mayo, May 5th is an important Mexican national holiday. It celebrates the Mexican victory over the French colonial troops in Puebla, Mexico on May 5, 1862. On St. Paul's West Side, Cinco de Mayo is celebrated over the closest weekend in May with an outdoor festival on Cesar Chavez (formerly Concord St.) Mexican bands, folk dancers and children's groups perform on five stages spread from Wabasha to Anita. Other activities include a community parade on Saturday at eleven, live Latin music, food and a children's area with face painting, storytelling, craft booths and more. This is a lively, colorful celebration of Hispanic culture and tradition.

*CIRCUSES - April

Everybody loves a circus! In the Twin Cities we are visited twice yearly by two different circuses. The St. Paul Osman Temple Shrine Circus (651-452-5662) **www.shrinecircus.com** performs in St. Paul in early April. In October, the Minneapolis Zuhrah Shrine Club Circus (612-871-3123) performs at the Target Center (612-673-9000) **www.targetcenter.com** and click on Event Calendar. Ticket prices vary from $10 to $25 with some local stores offering discount coupons. Contact the respective website or ticket office for information on admission fees, current locations and dates.

EARTH DAY - April

Founded in 1970 by Gaylord Nelson, former Wisconsin governor and U.S. senator, to educate people about the importance of protecting the environment. Officially E-Day is a Saturday in late April. However, events are held throughout the week leading up to E-Day. Activity announcements appear in the newspapers and as features on local TV newscasts. The website **www.earthday.org** also locates and provides details on scheduled programs and events in your area by searching on city or zipcode. Most are free with some having a small admission or ticket fee.

*FESTIVAL OF NATIONS - April & May
International Institute of Minnesota
1694 Como Ave.
St. Paul, 55108

651-647-0191
www.festivalofnations.com

This unique festival is an annual event held for four days Thursday through Sunday in late April into early May. It fills the St. Paul River-Centre on Kellogg Blvd. in St. Paul with as many as 90 ethnic groups coming from throughout Minnesota. People dressed in the costumes of their heritage set up booths of crafts for sale in the bazaar, have displays of their customs and culture in the exhibit area and sell foods of their heritage in the ethnic cafes. Programs of dance, song and music are continuous throughout the festival as are the many folk art demonstrations. It is best to locate a program immediately upon entering, select those events not to be missed and then just wander to discover. Admission is $10 for adults and $6 for children five to 16. Children under five are free when accompanied by an adult. Advance discount tickets are available.

Note: Student Group Days for grades six and up are Thursday and Friday. Special hours are set aside for the visits. Advance school group tickets are sold through the Festival of Nations office only.

*FLINT HILLS INTERNATIONAL CHILDREN'S FESTIVAL - May & June
Ordway Center for the Performing Arts
345 Washington St.
St. Paul, MN 55102

651-224-4222
www.ordway.org/festival

First held in 2001, this six-day festival for school groups and children with their family is located in and around Landmark Plaza in Rice Park in downtown St. Paul late May into early June. Primarily for ages five to 14, the festival is one of Ordway's efforts to provide more arts experiences for children. All activities, which adults will enjoy as well, include theater, music and dance, have international ties. Family Days are on Saturday and Sunday and School Days are on weekdays. Ticketed event prices are from $5.50 to $17.50. There are free outdoor festivities, too. Food for purchase is available.

MAYDAY PARADE & FESTIVAL - May
In the Heart of the Beast Puppet and Mask Theatre (HOBT)
1500 E. Lake St.
Minneapolis, 55407

612-721-2535
www.hobt.org

Each year a new theme is selected for this parade which features fantastic, giant puppets and masks. One year the theme was Leap into the Wonderous Possible. During the month of April, many of the masks and puppets are made in volunteer Tuesday and Thursday evening and Saturday workshops open to children and adults. The parade is always held on the first Sunday of May beginning at 1 PM on Bloomington Ave. S. and 25th St. It joyously travels to Powderhorn Park at 34th St and 15th Ave. S. where the festivities continue with puppet performances, music, food and the ceremony of the Rising of the Tree of Life. Call the theatre or visit its website for up-to-date details.

MEMORIAL DAY FESTIVAL - May
Lakewood Cemetery
3600 Hennepin Ave.
Hennepin Ave. S. & 36th St.
Minneapolis, 55408

612-822-2171
www.lakewoodcemetery.com

From morning to late afternoon, many activities are planned for families. Beginning with a traditional Memorial Day ceremony, visitors can go on to learn about cemetery lore. It could be cemetery symbols and art or family history. Each year the theme changes but is always educational. Did you know that a tulip is a declaration of love or sunflowers mean adoration? Gravestone-rubbings is one activity children can try. Carriage ride tours are offered. Live music can be enjoyed, too.

*MINNESOTA HORSE EXPO - April
State Fairgrounds
Como Ave. & Snelling
St. Paul, 55108

952-922-8666
www.mnhorseexpo.org

Sponsored by the Minnesota Horse Council, this discovered, close to home event, is held most often over the last weekend in April on the Minnesota State Fairgrounds. Over 300 horses are on display in the Sheep Barn. Clydesdales, Norwegian Fjords, Aztec and Miniatures are just a few of the breeds visitors can see and talk about with their owners and trainers. The Children's Area is in the Cattle Barn and includes such fun activities as trying to rope a pretend calf or groom a pony or cinch a saddle. Everyone is invited to enjoy the free horse carriage rides. A daily Parade of Breeds is held between 12:30 and 1 in the Coliseum Arena. And there are over 630 booths to browse among for horse products and services. Pick up a free schedule of events upon arrival. Admission is $8 for adults and $5 for seniors and children ages six to 12.

Note: The Minnesota Horse Council has a map of horse camping areas and horse trails throughout the State. For information on ordering a copy, call 763-754-3169 (infoline).

SHEPHERD'S HARVEST FESTIVAL & LLAMA MAGIC - May
Washington County Fairgrounds
Cty. Rd. 15 & State Hwy. 5
12300 N. 40 St.
Lake Elmo, 55042

www.shephersharvestfestival.org

This very special and unique event is really two. Held on Mother's Day weekend in May, the Shepherd's Harvest is a Sheep and Wool Festival with many planned children's activities including hands-on working with wool to make something, perhaps a bracelet, to take home. Each year a class for children is offered, too. One year it was felting on a bar of soap. Live animal demonstrations include sheepshearing and herding dogs. A delicious lamb burger or bratwurst lunch is available at a very modest cost. Try one before sold out as they go quickly. A variety of other kinds of foods are available for purchase, too.

Llama Magic is also family-oriented. At the show clinic, children as young as seven can learn how to handle a llama in the show ring. Children can take a llama for a walk around the fairgrounds. The llama and alpaca show is for spectators with the Llama Limbo, if scheduled, a must see.

Children's craft activities might include making a felt ball necklace from llama fiber.

SYTTENDE MAI (NORWEGIAN CONSTITUTION DAY) - May
Sons of Norway
1455 W. Lake St.
Minneapolis, 55408

612-827-3611
1-800-945-8851
www.sofn.com
www.mindekirken.org

Local Norwegians like to celebrate two days a year which have special meaning to them and friends of Norway. Syttende Mai is May 17th, Norway's Constitution Day. It is celebrated on the weekend closest to the 17th.

On Saturday in Loring Park at Yale Place and Willow in Minneapolis, the program and entertainment begin at noon with singing of the national anthem. Activities including demonstrations and performances follow. There is a parade, games for children, wood carving, rosemaling, singing, dancing and more.

On Sunday the festivities begin with the Syttende Mai Festival Service at 11 AM in the Norwegian Lutheran Memorial Church, 924 E. 21st St. in Minneapolis. This is followed by a meandering noon parade through the neighborhood ending at the church for refreshments, games for children and folk dancing. Contact the Sons of Norway or visit the websites for all the current details. Norway Day, the other special day, is celebrated in June and is included in the summer seasonal events.

Kom og kos deg med oss!
(Come and enjoy yourself with us!)

VETERINARY MEDICINE OPEN HOUSE - April
University of Minnesota
College of Veterinary Medicine
St. Paul Campus
1365 Gortner Ave.
St. Paul, 55108

612-624-4747
www.cvm.umn.edu

Annually held on a Sunday in early April from 11 AM to 4 PM, this is a day of fun and learning about animals and their medical care. Tours led by veterinary medicine students are offered. Children of ages eight and older will find the tour interesting as it is basically a walk through of the hospital. The examining rooms, surgery preparation area and pharmacies are shown. Children of all ages will enjoy seeing the live animal booths especially those with the dogs and small reptiles. Pamphlets and seminars are offered which teach and explain animal needs, rehabilitation and care.

Note: **The Raptor Center**, a short walk away, is open for free tours, also. See a description of the Raptor Center in the R's.

*WORLD WAR II AIR POWER DISPLAY - May
Commemorative Air Force (CAF)
Fleming Field Hanger 3
310 Airport Rd.
So. St. Paul, 55075

651-455-6942
www.cafsmw.org

The air show of the CFA's Minnesota Wing formerly held in August at Fleming Field is now held on Memorial Day weekend at the Red Wing Airport in Bay City, WI. With a display of over 30 different WW II restored aircraft including a B-25J Mitchell Medium Bomber and P51 Mustang, this event is well worth the short drive along the Mississippi River to their new location. People of all ages in our lucky community have the opportunity to have fun looking at the planes. The B29 Fifi and B24 Diamond Lil have been here. The huge C130 transport plane if available is a part of the show loaned by the National Guard. People can walk through it and see how really big it is! Usually an aircraft is available for rides at an additional cost. This is a very interesting event as the CAF volunteers are very proud of their aircraft and are very enthusiastic about sharing information and stories about each one.

Admission to the show is $15 for adults, $5 for children six to twelve and free for under six. A family package rate is also available. The admission fees collected are being used to restore and maintain the aircraft.

For more information, visit the website or call Wednesdays 10 AM to 6 PM or Saturdays between 10 AM and 5 PM to speak to one of the CFA volunteers. Ask about visiting their museum displays at Fleming Field. The museum visit is free and open to the public.

Note: Scouts, school groups and others can tour the aircraft restoration activity in Hanger 3 at Fleming Field in South St. Paul. It is very important to call 651-455-6942 ahead of time for reservations for the tour.

NOTES

SUMMER

AQUATENNIAL - July
Minneapolis Downtown Council
81 S. 9th St. Suite 260
Minneapolis, 55402

612-338-3807 or 612-376-7669 (infoline)
www.aquatennial.com

Beginning the third week in July, Minneapolis hosts their Ten Best Days of Summer festival honoring Minneapolis lakes and rivers. Many traditional family and youth events and activities are held during this celebration including the mid-week evening Torchlight Parade. Lake Calhoun is the location for the Milk Carton Boat Races, Sand Sculpturing and Sand Castle competition and sailing regatta. The end of the festival is concluded with a spectacular fireworks show launched over the Mississippi River. This is a celebration not to be missed. During the Aquatennial, the local newspapers list the daily events with their times and locations. A visit to the website provides events information as well.

CANADIAN DAYS - August
Little Canada City Center
515 Little Canada Rd. E.
Little Canada, 55117

651-766-4029
www.ci.little-canada.mn.us

Held over the first full weekend in August, this three day weekend celebration is at Spooner Park, Little Canada. Friday night is Corn Feed night. With the purchase of the child-designed Canadian Day button for $1, you receive two free ears of corn. Saturday the kiddie parade begins at 10 AM and features kiddie floats, wagons and children in costume. The parade starts at Little Canada Elementary School and goes one block to the park.

L. C.'s Playland returns each year. This is a penny carnival style playland with games and prizes. Other family events include carnival rides for all ages, a pancake breakfast, a Saturday night fireworks show and evening music for street dancing for all ages. The grand finale is the Grand Parade on Sunday at 1 PM.

DANISH DAY - June
Danish American Fellowship/Danebo
3030 W. River Pkwy. S.
Minneapolis, 55406

612-729-3800
www.danebo.org

All Danes look forward to this festival held the Sunday in June closest to Denmark's Constitution Day, June 5th. Held on the grounds of Danebo, folk dancing, Danish music, games and Danish craft and information booths are all a part of the celebration that begins with Danish pastries at 10:30 AM. Children of all ages can compete in Viking swordplay held in the Viking tent that has many Viking items on display, too. Open-faced sandwiches and other delicious Danish foods are available for sale. If the weather is uncooperative, some of the festival activities move into the building.

DEUTSCHER TAGE (GERMAN DAY) - June
Germanic-American Institute
301 Summit Ave.
St. Paul, 55102

651-222-7027 (infoline)
www.gai-mn.org

On the second weekend in June, Deutscher Tage is held at the Kulturhaus grounds on Summit Ave. from 11 AM to 6 PM. Schuhplattlers and Edelweiss dancers perform their special dances. German foods can be purchased to eat. There are singalongs, bands and more dancing. Booths are set-up displaying travel information about Germany and selling items having to do with Germany and German heritage. It's a fun time especially when a singalong gets started.

Note: The Kulturhaus House office is open from 1 to 5 PM on Mondays, Wednesdays, Fridays and 9 AM to 1 PM on Tuesdays, Thursdays. Special events and dinners are held throughout the year. Contact the Germanic-American Institute for information on these events, too.

GRAND OLD DAY - June
Grand Ave. Business Association
867 Grand Ave.
St. Paul, 55105
651-699-0029
www.grandave.com

Majestic Grand Avenue in the Summit Hill area of St. Paul is fun for families to explore during this celebration held on the first Sunday in June. The day's festivities start off with competitive inline skate and running races at 8 AM. A half mile youth run and walk/jog events are at 9 AM. The Children's Parade is at 10 AM with registration for it at 9:30. The Grand Old Day Parade begins at 10:30 AM at Dale and Grand and continues for several miles west along Grand to Fairview. A Family Fun area is setup in Ramsey Jr. High's parking lot at Grand and Wheeler. Entertainment continues all day for children and parents. Clowns, bands and other activities are planned to make the day fun for families. The day's activities end at 5 PM.

HIGHLAND FEST - July
Highland Business Association
790 Cleveland Ave. S. Suite 219
St. Paul, 55116
651-699-9042 (infoline)
www.highlandfest.com

During the third full weekend in July, this festival is held in the Highland Village neighborhood of St. Paul. Most activities take place around Ford Parkway and S. Cleveland Ave. Most children's activities are on Saturday between 10 AM and noon. In past years they have included pony rides, a petting zoo and face painting.

HIGHLAND PARK WATER TOWER - July
S.E. Corner of Snelling Ave. S. & Ford Pkwy.
St. Paul, 55116
651-266-6350
www.ci.stpaul.mn.us/depts/water/pages/events.html

For spectacular views of the Twin Cities, climb the 151 steps of this 127 foot tall historic and still operating water tower in July during Highland Fest. With a chair or bench on each of the many landings, even the smallest child can make the climb. The open-air observation deck has benches, too, for resting or for the young to stand on. The views from the top include the International Airport over 3 miles away, downtown Minneapolis 6 miles away and downtown St. Paul 4 miles. Very knowledgeable St. Paul Water Utility employees are present from 9 AM to 5 PM during the Open House event held during Highland Park's Highland Fest celebration. Postcards are for sale. Pamphlets on water quality and an "I saw St. Paul from the Top of the Highland Tower" sticker are free and can be picked up on the ground level.

IRISH FAIR OF MINNESOTA - August
Harriet Island in St. Paul
PO Box 2966
St. Paul, 55102

952-474-7411 (infoline)
www.irishfair.com

Held on the second full weekend in August, the fair has become one of the biggest celebrations of Irish culture in the Midwest. The Children's Area on the grounds provide lots of entertainment and activities for "the wee ones." Under a large tent covering many tables, clothespin doll dressing, picture painting and clay animals maybe crafted. Games, puppet shows, sheepdog demonstrations, music, dance and storytelling events are scheduled each day. Irish Soda bread is for sale.

The fair opens Friday with entertainment events at 5 PM, at 10 AM on Saturday and at 9 AM on Sunday for a church service followed by activities at 10:30 AM.

NORWAY DAY - July
Norwegian National League of Minnesota
7540 Edinborough Way #111
Edina, 55435

952-832-0164

This special day for Norwegians and friends is held on the second Sunday in July in Minnehaha Park. The event starts at 10 AM with a church service and continues with a Children's Flag Parade, Norwegian folk dancing, bands playing Norwegian music and booths set up typical of a small Norwegian fair. Refreshments featuring Scandinavian cookies and open-faced sandwiches are available.

RONDO DAYS FESTIVAL - July

Rondo Ave. Inc.
1360 University Ave. Suite 140
St. Paul, 55104

651-646-6597 (infoline)
www.rondodays.org

Held on the third Saturday in July, this is a reunion of sorts. The celebration activities are a way of carrying on the traditions of the former Rondo neighborhood, once the center of St. Paul's black community, that in the 1960's was eliminated with the construction of Hwy. 94. The former Rondo Road is now Concordia Ave. in St. Paul. Today, the day is filled with music of all types from the blues to hip-hop. Drill teams from many states compete at St. Paul Central's stadium. Other activities include the Rondo Days parade, musical performances and booths providing information on the community. Spicy ribs and corn on the cob are just a few of the tasty food items for sale. The festival is for people of all races, ages and communities. As the location varies, call Rondo Ave. Inc. or visit the website for the current year's location. And don't miss the fun!

ST. ANTHONY PARK ARTS FESTIVAL - June

Carter & Como Aves.
St. Paul, 55108

651-642-0411
www.stanthonyparkartsfestival.org

Traditionally held the first Saturday in June, this annual neighborhood event happens on Como from Carter to Luther Place in St. Anthony Park. The festival emphasizes books, crafts, food, and family entertainment. Children will have fun picking out books between the hours of 10 AM to 3 PM at the library's annual used book sale, eating ice cream treats, listening to musical entertainment and watching a magic show or street corner juggler. A Children's Art Activity Tent is set-up at Luther Place. Adults will enjoy the many craft stalls on the lawns of the library and Luther Seminary and browsing through the bookbins of Micawber's. Look for Speedy Market's food wagon for their special brats, hot dogs, burgers and drinks. Good eats at reasonable prices. The festival is from 9:30 AM to 5:30 PM.

SVENSKARNAS DAG /SWEDISH HERITAGE DAY - June
www.SvenskarnasDag.com

The Swedish residents (and non-Swedish who want to attend) gather each year on the last Sunday in June in Minnehaha Park to celebrate with a morning church service, raising of the Midsommar Pole, dancing, music and enjoying Swedish foods. The highlight of the day is the crowning of the Midsommar Queen during the afternoon program. For more information on the day's activities, visit the website.

TASTE OF MINNESOTA - July
1097 Payne Ave.
St. Paul, 55101

651-772-9980
www.tasteofmn.org

This is a food tasting festival held at Harriet Island in St. Paul for four to five days in early July always including the fourth. Primarily for adults to sample specialty dishes of local restaurants, a section of the grounds called KidZone is set aside for children's entertainment activities. These might include face painting, story times, a craft area, a toy play tent, mini-golf, and the KidZone Stage with variety acts such as dancing, magicians and visiting zoo animals. Especially nice for parents with very young children is the diaper changing tent. The hours for these activities are 11 AM to 9 PM each day. Admission to the grounds is free.

NOTES

FALL

ANOKA HALLOWEEN PARADES - October
PO Box 385
Anoka, 55303

763-427-1861
www.anokahalloween.com/index.htm

Halloween capitol of the world, Anoka holds a big week long event with three parades to celebrate this time of the year. The Light Up the Night parade is the first and is held on the next to last Saturday at 7 PM on Main Street. The Big Parade of Little People is at 1:15 PM on the following Friday and includes elementary school children in costume and the junior high school marching bands. The next day, the Saturday parade, a gigantic extravaganza of marching bands, clowns, queens, animals and all sorts of marvelous floats parades down Main St. beginning at 1 PM and lasting two hours. Other activities held during the week long festivities include foot races for all family members and the Queen's Pageant. Another continuing tradition is the Big Haunted House sponsored by the Knights of Columbus and held at the Anoka County Fairgrounds. For all the historical details, Pat Ward has for 35 years been a good contact reachable evenings at 763-421-5086.

Note: Look for Key Dates on their website for all the event details.

BOO BASH - October
Grand Ave. Business Association
867 Grand Ave.
St. Paul, 55105

651-699-0029
www.grandave.com/boo_bash.htm

A new event on Grand Ave., the Boo Bash, is for families who like to celebrate Halloween together by dressing up in costume and meandering the avenue to gather treats. The little ones with the Moms, the Dads and even some family pets in costume enjoy the activities between 10 AM and 2 PM on the Saturday before Halloween. Besides the goodies given out by local businesses, there are horse-drawn hay wagon rides, free pumpkins at the Pumpkin Patch and pet and children's costume contests. This event is fun to see as well as participate in.

CARNIVAL OF THE ARTS - October
Edina Art Center
4701 W. 64th St.
Edina, 55435

612-915-6600
www.EdinaArtCenter.com

This is a Free Family Fun Day event held on a Sunday afternoon early in October. Hands-on children's art activities, artist demonstrations, refreshments and performances by local talent make this a most enjoyable event for all ages. Visit their website or call for the current date and details.

*CIRCUSES - October

Everybody loves a circus! In the Twin Cities we are visited twice yearly by two different circuses. The St. Paul Osman Temple Shrine Circus (651-452-5662) **www.shrinecircus.com** performs in St. Paul in early April. In October, the Minneapolis Zuhrah Shrine Club Circus (612-871-3555) **www.zuhrah.org** performs at the Target Center (612-673-1313) **www.targetcenter.com** and click on Event Calendar. Ticket prices vary from $10 to $25 with some local stores offering discount coupons. Contact the respective website or ticket office for information on admission fees, current locations and dates.

CZECHOSLOVAK DAY - September
CSPS Hall
West 7 St. & Western Ave.
383 Michigan St.
St. Paul, 55102

651-290-0542 (infoline)

The second Saturday in September is for celebrating Czechoslovakian heritage. The event begins with a noon parade and continues until 5 PM with music, food, games, dancing and singing. Food includes ethnic goodies like Czech Booya and sausages as well as American favorites. There are craft booths and displays too. For more the information about this special day, call 612-920-5949.

HIGHLAND PARK WATER TOWER - October
S.E. Corner of Snelling Ave. S. & Ford Pkwy.
St. Paul, 55116

651-266-6350
www.stpaul.gov/depts/water/NewsEvents.htm

Climb the 151 steps of this 127 foot tall historic and still operating water tower the second weekend in October for the beautiful fall foliage views. With a chair or bench on each landing every 15 to 20 steps, even the smallest child can make the climb. The observation deck has benches, too, for resting or for the young to stand on. The views from the top include the International Airport over 3 miles away, downtown Minneapolis 6 miles away and downtown St. Paul 4 miles. Very knowledgeable St. Paul Water Utility employees are on duty from 9 AM to 5 PM during the tower's Fall Open House. Postcards are for sale. Pamphlets on water quality are free. And an "I saw St. Paul from the Top of the Highland Tower" sticker is your reward when returning to ground level.

*RENAISSANCE FESTIVAL - August & September
Mid-America Festivals
1244 S. Canterbury Rd. Suite 306
Shakopee, 55379

952-445-7361
1-800-966-8215 (infoline)
www.renaissancefest.com

The festival offers many fascinating things for everyone of all ages. It is the recreation of a 16th century celebration complete with authentically costumed musicians, dancers, mimes, cooks, beggars and other characters of the time. There are craftsmen in thatched huts demonstrating and selling the making of their wares. Games of skill like archery and fencing, King's Joust and the Queens Darts can be tried. Daily special events include authentic real armored jousting, strolling minstrels, puppeteers and magicians. Everywhere there is food to purchase like Scotch eggs, corn on the cob, roasted sausages and cheeses and breads.

Located 4 miles south of Shakopee on Highway 169, the festival is open 9 AM to 7 PM weekends and Labor Day from mid-August through late September. Parking and all entertainment are included in the admission fee that is $18.95 for adults, $16.95 for seniors, $9.95 for children ages six through 12 and free for children five and under.

*STATE FAIR - August & September
Midway Pkwy. & Snelling Ave.
1265 Snelling Ave. N.
Falcon Heights, 55108
651-288-4400
www.mnstatefair.org

This is one of the largest fairs in the nation. Held for twelve days, it starts the last week of August and always ends on Labor Day. On designated Kids Days, children five to twelve are admitted for $4. Children will find many things of interest at the fair including the cattle barns, horse barns, machinery hill, and the activities and displays in the education, natural resources and 4-H buildings. Children have their own animal barnyard at the Children's FFA Barnyard. Not to be missed is the Children's Theater Stage where the attractions are planned for families. The show might include a juggler, science show, flea circus or magician. The shows last about 30 minutes, are free and are repeated throughout each day.

Take a least one ride down the Giant Slide. Have a least one corn dog. And share a bag of mini donuts.

Gate admission to the fair is $9 for adults. Children five to twelve and seniors 65 and older are admitted for $8. Tickets purchased in advance are discounted. Children under five are free. The gates open at 6 AM and close at 10 PM. Most exhibit building hours are 9 to 9 daily. Parking on the fairgrounds is $9.

NOTES

WINTER

BLACK HISTORY CELEBRATIONS

The months of January and February offer opportunities to learn about black leaders and black history through many community events and activities.

Celebrate the Dream, a tribute to Martin Luther King Jr., is an event held at the Basilica of St. Mary **www.mary.org** on Hennepin Ave. S. in Minneapolis each year on Dr. King's January 15th birthdate. The free evening event includes music, humanitarian awards and a keynote address. For additional information visit the website or call 612-333-1381.

The Science Museum of Minnesota **www.ssm.org** holds **African Americans Science Day** on a Saturday in February. The event provides children the opportunity to do science projects with local scientist and engineers. Reservations required (651-221-9444).

The Martin Luther King Center **www.hqbcc.org** 270 Kent St. in St. Paul (651-224-4601) participates with other organizations in activities including the free **Rev. Martin Luther King, Jr. Holiday Breakfasts** usually held in local churches. These community breakfasts, which require reservations, begin at 7 AM. At 8 AM the event's keynote speaker's address is broadcasted live to all locations. Visit **www.mlkbreakfast.org** in late December or call for details.

*A CHRISTMAS CAROL - November & December
Guthrie Theater
818 2nd   St. S.
Minneapolis, 55415

612-377-2224
1-877-44STAGE
www.guthrietheater.org

Charles Dickens' A CHRISTMAS CAROL has become a holiday tradition play for over 30 years now. Older children will understand and enjoy the play that is performed from mid-November through December. The costumes, stage setting and special effects as well as the acting are always outstanding. When Marley's ghost ascends from below stage in a cloud of misty smoke, everyone in the audience shudders as he moans and his chains clink. Scrooge is wonderfully transitioned from a greedy miser to a generous uncle throughout the production. This is a very popular seasonal treat with tickets becoming available for purchase as early as September. Call or visit the website for performance dates and times and ticket prices that range from $25 to $55.

*FAMILY CONCERTS - February & March & April
Music in the Park Series
2255 Doswell Ave. Suite 201
St. Paul, 55108

651-645-5699
www.musicinthepartkseries.org

Three different concerts are held each winter series. Children along with their family members will enjoy listening to and participating in the folk, ethnic and classical performances of the children friendly artists.

In a large room with children seated on the floor up close to the performers and adults seated in back on folding chairs or standing holding the younger ones, the concert begins with introductions. Then there are the reminders to listen with your ears and look with your eyes and move to the rythmns.

As the concert continues, children maybe invited to come forward and participate in making music. This produces lots of smiles.

Concerts are Friday evenings at 6:15 and repeated at 7:30 at St. Matthew's Episcopal Church in St. Anthony Park, 2136 Carter Ave., St. Paul. Season tickets are $12. Single tickets are $5 in advance and $6 at the door. However, as the concerts are very popular and often sold out, it is best to purchase in advance.

GERMAN CHRISTMAS CELEBRATION - November or December
Germanic-American Institute (GAI)
301 Summit Ave.
St. Paul, 55102

651-222-7027
www.gai-mn.org/index.html

On a Sunday afternoon in late November or early December, the German Kulturhaus on Summit Ave. holds Open Haus from 11 AM to 4 PM. The Volksfest Singers give a concert of German Christmas carols. And visitors are invited to join in the singing. Other activities include tours of the house beautifully decked out with wreaths, tinsel and Christmas trees featuring traditional decorations like candy canes and candles.

GRAND MEANDER - December
Grand Ave. Business Association
867 Grand Ave.
St. Paul, 55105

651-699-0029
www.grandave.com/grand-meander.htm

On the first Saturday in December from 8:30 AM to the early evening hours, the Grand Ave. merchants invite families to spend the day exploring the avenue. There one can find a breakfast with Santa, Christmas carolers, free soup tastings, holiday characters, Santa's reindeer, roasted chestnuts and free horse-drawn hayrides. Also catch a free ride on the Grand Avenue Express, a Victorian-style trolley powered by natural gas. Sounds like fun. It is. Bundle up and enjoy the day.

HOLIDAZZLE PARADES - November & December
Minneapolis Downtown Council
81 S. 9th St. Suite 260
Minneapolis, 55402

612-338-3807
www.holidazzle.com

This holiday tradition is held on Nicollet Mall from late November through December Wednesday through Sunday evenings each week beginning at 6:30 PM. The parade winds down Nicollet Mall for 30 minutes. Each parade is different. Lighted floats, musical groups and other surprises entertain the parade watchers. One might see a lighted 60-foot Chinese dragon or Santabear in a sleigh. A very family-oriented event featuring nursery rhyme and storybook costumed entertainers, this is a delightful parade we hope continues for a long time. And of course Santa Claus always makes an appearance. One of the sponsors of the parades is the Minneapolis Downtown Council. For more information, contact them at 612-376-SNOW or visit the website.

*JAPANESE NEW YEAR CELEBRATION - January
The Japan America Society of Minnesota (JASM) celebrates the new year with this family festival to which everyone is invited. The party is generally held on the Sunday before Martin Luther King Jr.'s birthday at William Mitchell College of Law, 875 Summit Ave., from 4 to 8 PM. There is typically Japanese drumming performances, artists demonstrating Japanese cartoon drawing called manga and special games for children as well as traditional music and dance. Admission is $20 for a family package, $8

for adults and $5 for seniors and students. Children five and younger are free. For current date and details, contact JASM at 612-627-9357 or visit their website at **www.mn-japan.org**

*KWANZAA FAMILY CELEBRATION - December
Minnesota History Center (MHC)
345 Kellogg Blvd. W.
St. Paul, 55102

651-296-6126
1-800-657-3773
www.mnhs.org

Beginning on December 26 and continuing for six more days, Kwanzaa is an American holiday season created in 1966 to celebrate African culture through traditional music, stories and the arts. Kwanzaa, a Swahili word, means "first." And so on the first day of the festival, the MHC each year plans an afternoon of family events. These could include storytelling, dance, drumming and always a hands-on African themed children's art activity. One year it was creating a linguist staff from cardboard paper rolls, beads, colored tissues, tapes and trinkets. Admission is $8 for adults, $6 for seniors and $4 for children from six to 17. The Minnesota Café located in the MHC serves Kwanzaa themed food, too.

MACY'S CHILDREN'S EVENTS - November & December
700 Nicollet Mall
Minneapolis, 55402

612-375-3018
www.macys.com

A traditional holiday show in the store's 8th floor auditorium opens about mid-November and continues through December. The 10,000 square-foot area is transformed into a fantasyland of imaginative settings and animated characters with the visitors to it looking and listening as they walk through the show. A different theme is planned each year. Recent shows have included Cinderella, Snow White and Charlie & the Chocolate Factory.

On certain days during the holiday season, children can have Breakfast with Santa and his Friends for $15 at the stores with restaurants. Call for dates or visit the website.

Another annual event for children and parents is the popular Easter-time Bunny Breakfast for $15.

Note: A ten-day flower show held in March co-sponsored by Bachman's is mainly for adults but most children enjoy a short walk-through visit, too. Music in the Garden: An Interactive Musical Journey was the theme of a previous show. Go during the less crowded evening hours or early Saturday morning.

*MINNESOTA FILM ARTS - December
University of Minnesota
Minneapolis Campus
Bell Auditorium
University Ave. & 17th Ave. S.E.
Minneapolis, 55455

612-331-7563 or 612-331-3134 (infoline)
www.mnfilmarts.org

In the week following Christmas, Minnesota Film Arts (formerly the U Film Society) has traditionally shown the film Ronya, the Robber's Daughter based on the Astrid Lindgren novel. To receive more information, visit their website or contact them directly. Admission is $4 for adults and $4 for children.

*NORTHWEST SPORTSHOW - March
Minneapolis Convention Center
1301 S. 2nd Ave.
Minneapolis, 55403

612-335-6000 or 612-335-6025 (infoline)
www.mplsconvctr.org
www.NorthwestSportshow.com

This show has been an annual event for over 70 years, but in recent years has become a truly family event. Changes have taken place to include entertainment and activities for young visitors. Children can learn more about the outdoors, indoors, as they are encouraged to learn about fishing, hunting safely and bird watching.

Held for a week beginning in late March, the show has included a trout pond where a child can fish keeping the catch or returning it to the pond. They can discover the fun of fly fishing by learning to tie a fly and how to fly cast. Admission is $9 for adults, $4 for youth 13 to 15 and free for children twelve and under. Look for discount coupons available at some local stores.

*THE NUTCRACKER

With many fine Nutcracker ballet productions to choose from presently, a time to attend a performance of this seasonal family treat should be found during even the busiest of December weekends.

The story told begins with a magician bringing toys to children at a Christmas party. Clara receives a nutcracker that later that night comes to life. She then helps him lead the toy soldiers to victory over the invading mice. The nutcracker becomes a prince who then takes Clara to the Kingdom of Sweets for dancing and to be entertained by the Sugar Plum Fairy.

And any one of these productions will provide the same wonderful enchanting entertainment for children of all ages.

*Ballet Minnesota's **The Classic Nutcracker** (651-290-0513) is the traditional version of the ballet with guest dancers from well-known ballet companies. Children's roles are danced by our local Classical Ballet Academy students. Performances are in mid-December at O'Shaughnessy, College of St. Catherine, 2004 Randolph Ave., St. Paul, 55105, (651-690-6700). Tickets are $12 to $35. **www.balletminnesota.org**

*Loyce Houlton's Nutcracker Fantasy** has been a favorite for over 40 years. The New York Times has called the Minnesota Dance Theatre's (MDT) (612-338-0627) production one of the ten best American Nutcrackers. Performances are held in mid-December at the Historic State Theatre, 805 Hennepin Ave., Minneapolis, 55402, (612-673-0404). Tickets are $11.50 to $44. **www.mndance.org/site**

*Stillwater Nutcracker** is also a traditional performance. However, it has narration that makes it more understandable and enjoyable for younger children. Professional dancers perform with hundreds of St. Croix Ballet students some as young as five. Performances are the last weekend in November and the first weekend in December at the Stillwater Area High School Auditorium, 5701 Stillwater Blvd. N., Oak Park Heights, 55082, (651-439-2820). Tickets are $12. **www.stcroixballet.com**

PHILIPPINE DAY - March
Rice Park
Landmark Center
75 W. 5 St.
St. Paul, 55102

651-292-3225 (infoline)
www.landmarkcenter.org

On a Sunday afternoon in late March, Philippine food, folk music and dance can be enjoyed at the Landmark Center. The festival is sponsored by the Cultural Society of Filipino Americans in the Twin Cities. Arts and crafts are for sale and there are interesting exhibits, too.

ST. PATRICK'S DAY PARADE & CELEBRATION - March
St. Patrick's Day Association
PO Box 2303
St. Paul, 55102

651-256-2155 (infoline)
www.stpatsassoc.org

St. Patrick's Day is March 17th and is celebrated in St. Paul with a Walking Parade. The St. Paul organizers think only New York City and Boston have larger parades than ours. However, they fondly think of ours as the largest Baby Buggy parade. This is a family event with children riding in decorated wagons and baby strollers. In fact, anyone can march in the parade as long as he or she is wearing something green.

However, advance registration is required by the association to participate in the parade. The registration form is available on their website.

In a recent parade, the O'Any Bodies family marched. And a grade school kazoo band could be heard playing When Irish Eyes Are Smiling.

In St. Paul, the parade starts about noon and winds through the downtown area. Consult their website or the St. Paul newspaper for the parade route and starting time.

*SCOTTISH RAMBLE - February
Rice Park
Landmark Center
75 W. 5th St.
St. Paul, 55102

651-292-3225 (infoline)
www.scottishramble.org

On a weekend in February, our local Scottish heritage is promoted with pipe bands, Celtic music and highland dances. Children are encouraged to sit near the performance stage and have been known to enjoy the music so much they stand up and start dancing, too. And this is fine with the performers.

There are displays of bagpipes, Scottish customs and clan information. Scottish food and crafts are sold. Admission is $5 for adults and $3 for seniors and children.

*SHAKESPEARE CLASSIC - January
Guthrie Theater
818 2nd St. S.
Minneapolis, 55415

612-372-2244
www.guthrietheatreplace.org

During the school year and during a Guthrie production of a Shakespeare play, children accompanied by an adult can attend a one-time, annual special matinee performance. In the past, the performance has been on a Sunday in January or March or April. The event month is dependent upon when the Guthrie schedules their Shakespeare play. Tickets are available three months in advance, are only $5 each and go quickly. This is a way to introduce families to the wonderful world of live theater at our Guthrie.

Older children will especially enjoy and understand the play with some beforehand preparation. An excellent brochure containing program notes especially written for young people is mailed out when tickets are purchased. The program is given out in the theater lobby on the day of performance, also. Be sure to read through it before the play begins to learn about the story and characters. Following the play, children are invited to meet the actors. Refreshments are served, too. Visit the Guthrie website for an announcement of when the Shakespeare Classic program is to be held each year.

URBAN EXPEDITIONS - January - April
Rice Park
Landmark Center
75 W. 5th St.
St. Paul, 55102

651-292-3276
www.landmarkcenter.org

Children experience the cultures of countries outside the United States without leaving S. Paul at Urban Expeditions. Each child is given a passport at his or hers first visit to this event. It can then be used for "entrance" to future visits. On select Sundays at 1 PM January through April, the music and dance and an art activity of a different country is explored. Past countries visited have included Jamaica, Greece and Japan. Call or check website for specific future dates and countries scheduled for travel.

WINTER CARNIVAL - January
St. Paul Festival & Heritage Foundation
429 Landmark Center
75 W. 5th St.
St. Paul, 55102

651-223-4700 (infoline)
www.winter-carnival.com

The first Winter Carnival was held in 1886 as a celebration of the end of winter and the beginning of spring. Each year since, Vulcan on the last day of the carnival tries to dethrone King Boreas to bring about spring-like weather. The fiery Vulcan always wins but warm weather never arrives as predicted by his victory. Another tradition at each year's carnival is the spectacular ice carving competition now held on Harriet Island.

Events children might like to participate in include the medallion treasure hunt, ice maze and snow slide.

Winter Carnival activities begin the last Friday in January and continue through the following week ending on Saturday. In 2007, the traditional Grande Day and Torchlight parades merged into one "day-into-night" parade that concludes with a fireworks display on the final Saturday. In the parade, the popular Hi-lex bleach gnomes marching unit, fondly known as the drips of bleach, receive lots of cheers.

This is the oldest winter celebration in North America and we really enjoy it! Check local newspapers or visit their website for all the many scheduled official events and their current locations.

NOTES

CATEGORIES INDEX

Animals

Art Activities & Centers

Birthday Parties

Camps & Classes

Fairs & Festivals

Film Programs

Flower Gardens & Shows

Heritage & Nationality Culture

Historical Sites & Societies

Libraries

Museums

Music

Nature Centers & Programs

Observation Decks & Platforms

Parades

Parks & Recreational Centers

Playgrounds

Puppet Shows & Storytime Programs

Sports

Theaters & Shows

Tours

Transportation & Rides